When I Was a
Turkey

When I Was a Turkey

BASED ON THE EMMY AWARD–WINNING
PBS DOCUMENTARY
MY LIFE AS A TURKEY

Joe Hutto

with Brenda Z. Guiberson
illustrations by Joe Hutto

Christy Ottaviano Books
Henry Holt and Company • New York

Henry Holt and Company, *Publishers since 1866*
Henry Holt® is a registered trademark of Macmillan Publishing Group, LLC
175 Fifth Avenue, New York, NY 10010
mackids.com

Library of Congress Cataloging-in-Publication Data

Names: Hutto, Joe. | Guiberson, Brenda Z.
Title: When I was a turkey : based on the Emmy award–winning PBS documentary My life as
    a turkey / Joe Hutto with Brenda Z. Guiberson.
Description: New York : Henry Holt and Company, 2017.
Identifiers: LCCN 2017026781 (print) | LCCN 2017007364 (ebook) |
    ISBN 9781627793865 (Ebook) | ISBN 9781627793858 (hardback)
Subjects: LCSH: Wild turkey–Behavior–Juvenile literature. | Human-animal
    relationships–Juvenile literature. | Imprinting (Psychology)–Juvenile literature. |
    Hutto, Joe–Juvenile literature.
Classification: LCC QL696.G254 (print) | LCC QL696.G254 H874 2017 (ebook) |
    DDC 598.6/45–dc23
LC record available at https://lccn.loc.gov/2017026781

Our books may be purchased in bulk for promotional, educational, or business use.
Please contact your local bookseller or the Macmillan Corporate and
Premium Sales Department at (800) 221-7945 ext. 5442 or by e-mail at
MacmillanSpecialMarkets@macmillan.com.

First edition, 2017 / Designed by Patrick Collins
Printed in the United States of America by LSC Communications, Harrisonburg, Virginia.

1 3 5 7 9 10 8 6 4 2

For my father Joe N. Hutto (Sr.)
who ignited my interest in the natural world.
—J. H.

For Jason, Heather, and PJ,
all learning new things and curious about everything.
—B. Z. G.

Contents

Foreword

THIS PROJECT BEGAN a number of years ago as an ordinary science experiment. After receiving some orphaned wild turkey eggs, I set about the task of hatching the eggs and trying to become the parent to over twenty baby birds through the process of imprinting. The experiment became more time consuming, physically difficult, and emotionally challenging than I could have ever imagined. We lived together in the wilderness for well over a year! I documented the project in a daily journal, which included the drawings in this book.

Nature always proves to be more interesting and complicated than we expect. As a naturalist and anthropologist, I am familiar with uncovering the science behind experiments in nature. What I didn't expect was that I'd find such an intriguing new family among the wild turkeys; together we shared a world of excitement and wonder. This is my story. I hope you enjoy it.

When I Was a Turkey

CHAPTER 1

Talking Turkey

ANIMALS EVERYWHERE!

AS A CHILD, Joe Hutto had every kind of pet imaginable. His parents put linoleum on his bedroom floor and said he could keep almost any critter in his bedroom or outside as long as he kept it clean and well fed. The big rule was no poisonous snakes. Growing up in Florida Joe kept birds, mammals, and reptiles, and most of them slept with him in his bed. At one point he had a small bobcat, a seven-foot boa constrictor (not poisonous), and a gray squirrel all living peacefully in his room.

Joe always wanted to be around as many wild animals as possible. When he was twelve and alone in a misty forest, his whole body tingled when he called to a wild turkey and it snuck up close to him. As a college student, he studied with wildlife biologists. As an archaeologist, he examined animal bones and stomach contents. As a naturalist, he spent long hours in camouflage to learn about wild turkeys and wood ducks. As a wildlife artist, he drew beautiful details. As a trainer, he worked with dogs and horses. As a wrangler, he captured snakes for zoos. But with all his various activities, he rarely got to look at animals in the wild for more than a few minutes.

In 1991, Joe and his wife, Claudia, a teacher in the local gifted program, were living in an old house on a Florida plantation. Tractor drivers there were preparing a swampy area for better quail habitat. They had a hard time seeing into the tall plants on the ground, and they were unintentionally disrupting wild turkey hens on their nests and destroying eggs.

Joe saw an incredible opportunity if he could get some of those eggs. He asked the tractor drivers to bring him any they might save.

Joe had unusual plans for these eggs. He was eager to explore the mystery of what it means to be wild, to see if he could find a window into the secret life of these turkeys. He wanted the new hatchlings to imprint on him, to regard him as their real "mother," since no hen would be around to care for them. He had tried imprinting before with wood ducks and other creatures, but now it seemed like he had an incredible opportunity to get very close to wild turkeys and learn more about them.

He didn't expect to get any eggs, but still he waited and checked and waited some more.

EGGS DELIVERED

ON MAY 3, a stainless-steel bowl showed up on Joe's doorstep. It was full of wild-turkey eggs. They were bigger than chicken eggs, smooth and bone-colored with small brown flecks. Suddenly Joe was a wild-turkey parent, and the 16 eggs before him needed focused attention.

With no hen to gather them close, the eggs were already getting cold. All tasks of incubation and protection now belonged to Joe. Could he do it? Could he be the "mother"? And what would that mean?

Joe acted quickly. For warmth, he rushed them to the top of a hot-water heater and covered them with towels. He added a bit of water so they wouldn't get too dry. Then he raced to a neighbor's house to borrow an incubator. He also got some advice. Keep the eggs at 99.5°F with the humidity at 85 percent. Mark each egg with a small dot and turn it twice a day. Otherwise the yolk will stick to the inside of the shell and the embryo will die.

Joe worked hard for hours. He lined the incubator and the shelf it was on with towels. The rough towel texture would be better than a smooth surface to keep the young hatchlings, called poults, from slipping when they walked. A fall could permanently damage their leg tendons, and they would never be able to stand. This condition is called "spraddle leg."

Then he used a technique called "candling" to find out which eggs were fertile and would hatch. To do this, Joe observed each egg in front of a strong light. In 15 eggs, he could see a dark shape inside, which was the embryo. The 16th egg had no dark shape: It was infertile and contained no embryo.

About 1:00 A.M. the 15 fertile eggs finally were marked and laid out in neat rows in the warm incubator. They were in a storage room with no windows, so Joe used a fan to keep the air circulating. He was exhausted but so excited too. Right in front of him he had wild turkey eggs and a rare chance to really connect with them.

EGGSITTING

THE NEXT DAY, Joe stared in wonder at the beautiful eggs, in awe of the potential inside each one. He knew that turkey eggs hatch after 25 days, but he didn't know exactly how old these were. They were filled with embryos developing cell by cell, step by step, into a mystery he had always wanted to explore: wildness. The wild turkey. As the responsible and caring eggsitter, he found himself spending hours at a time with them. But he wondered, was he doing everything right? How many would survive? What would they need? And would he be ready?

When he could tear himself away from the eggs, he bought a waterer and a 50-pound bag of turkey "starter" feed that was a nutritious mix of vitamins, minerals, and protein. He also picked up two Rhode Island Red chickens. Somewhere he had heard that chickens should be around to teach new turkeys to peck. But Joe felt that this was an insult to wild turkeys everywhere. Did they really need to be taught this behavior?

Two days later, an embryo died. He detected a smell of sulfur when he came into the room. He felt terrible and worried about the 14 remaining eggs. Were they healthy enough? He hoped that at least a few would hatch so that he could live in the world of wild creatures from the very beginning.

DOUBLE DUTY ON EGGS

ON MAY 7, Joe got a second delivery of 14 more eggs from a different nest. The driver reported that unfortunately the hen had been killed by the mower, and at least one egg had been broken with a well-formed young turkey inside. Some eggs were stained with splotches of blood, which needed to be removed immediately so the eggs could breathe.

Joe didn't take time to candle this new batch by observing their developemental stage in front of a bright light but cleaned and marked each egg with a small dot. He placed them all on a separate rack in the incubator, where they could be safe and warm with the other eggs.

In his notes, he referred to the first group as clutch #1 and this new group that seemed more developed as clutch #2.

Now he was a busy, busy parent of 28 eggs. Twice a day he turned each one. He observed, listened, and sniffed. Taking only brief periods for eating and sleeping, he stayed with them as much as possible. But he didn't stay quietly.

TALKING TURKEY

JOE COULD IMITATE SOUNDS with his voice that wild turkeys make. While the little chicks grew inside the shells, he spoke to them in both "Turkey" and English. He was a bit embarrassed and did this secretly when no one was around. He felt the eggs from the advanced clutch #2 were definitely listening, and soon he was talking quietly every hour or two. He *purred*, *trilled*, *putt-putted*, and spoke English to let them get used to his voice. The poults responded to him with *peep peep peep!* This back-and-forth gave the growing chicks an early introduction to Joe, just as they would have heard a wild turkey hen and learned to recognize her voice.

As he *purred* and *trilled*, Joe wondered if the turkeys would ever hatch. And when should he stop turning the eggs? After 25 days, the birds wouldn't need more rotation because they could turn themselves. Then they would start to "pip," or peck the first tiny hole in the shell. Turkeys have a special projection on their beak called an "egg tooth," which lasts a day or two, solely for this purpose. They also have a temporary hatching muscle on the back of their head that helps them bang the egg tooth against the inside of the shell.

Joe didn't know when day 25 would arrive but the growing turkeys did. Wild turkeys have been around for 20 million years and the chicks had the wisdom of the ages to know when to pip.

PIP, CRACK, HATCH!

ON FRIDAY, MAY 10, a tiny hole the size of a pinhead appeared on an egg in clutch #2. The first chick had pipped! Joe turned off the fan and gently talked in Turkey and English. For the first time he could hear faint *kee kee kees* coming from the eggs. Were they talking to him? He *yelped* and again heard a mumbled response of *kees*. Back and forth, Joe *yelped* and listened to the wonderful faint chorus that answered. When they took a rest, Joe closed the incubator and restarted the fan. But he kept checking.

He waited and watched for three more hours. At last the first turkey to pip started to bite around the tiny hole. Using its egg tooth and extra head muscle, it chipped out a larger and larger crack in the shell. Joe cheered it on with turkey pep talks. The hardworking bird made more cracks, and more, and finally broke out of the shell. The whole chipping process took 55 minutes and the little poult emerged wet, weak, and wobbly.

Joe was so excited to see the first one that he hardly knew what to do. Finally he remembered to talk softly to the new arrival. He *yelped* softly like a hen.

The wobbly little turkey turned toward him. It looked him straight in the eye. It was an incredible moment, a newly hatched turkey staring intensely into the eye of the first living thing it saw. It was a magical look, one that could not be ignored.

Joe didn't know it yet but this look, and more like it, would take all of his attention for the next two years and change him for the rest of his life.

CHAPTER 2

Look Me in the Eye

THE POWER OF IMPRINTING

JOE HELD THE FIRST little poult close to his face. It *purr purred*, cuddled against his cheek, and seemed comfortable. When it fell asleep, he put it gently back into the incubator. Joe kept a close watch as two more eggs pipped from clutch #2.

Since there was no hatching activity he eventually turned out the light and went back to the house to go to bed. But how could he sleep? He worried about the poult that had hatched, the ones that had pipped, and all the others waiting for their moment in the incubator. He set the alarm and checked them several times during the night. He found more pipped eggs, but only from clutch #2. There was no activity in clutch #1.

As the sun rose on Saturday, May 11, Joe rushed back to the incubator. The yellow-and-brown hatchling from the day before was now fluffy and dry and very, very cute. When it saw Joe, it relaxed and stumbled right over to him. Since Joe was the first living thing it had seen and then looked him directly in the eye, the poult recognized and responded to Joe as its mother. This is the process called imprinting.

Imprinting is an unchangeable bond that happens with many creatures. It is especially strong in fowl like turkeys, chickens, quail, and pheasant. These types of birds are precocial, born with feathers, open eyes, and an ability to walk from the very first moments. They don't lie around in the nest waiting to be fed. They are up and about right away and must find a mother quickly to help them survive.

Joe, already a mother to one, was delighted to see two newly hatched wet turkeys and a third that was almost out of the shell. In the darkness, these poults had not yet seen any other living thing. Now if they lifted their droopy heads, they would see Joe. Would he then become their mother too?

Joe stood near the incubator and quietly *yelped* and *purred*. The three newcomers turned toward him, stared into his eyes, and stumbled across the towel in his direction. When they reached the edge of the shelf, he held all four in his hand. They cuddled against his cheek. They and Joe filled the room with soft *trills* and *peeps* until the poults fell asleep.

They were firmly imprinted on Joe. In this quick eye communication, he became their object of devotion. For Joe it was such a deep and intense connection that he could hardly describe it.

OUT OF THE INCUBATOR
AND INTO THE BROODER

ALL DAY LONG, Joe was busy, busy, busy. He removed broken shell pieces from the incubator and replaced the dirty towels. He checked each egg and made sure every pip hole was turned to the top. The eggs with holes were all in clutch #2, although four eggs were still not active. None of the eggs in clutch #1 had yet pipped. He was getting more worried about them. Were they growing as they should?

He checked on the new poults. They were asleep in a downy pile. Through the afternoon, he watched six more turkeys break out of their shells, react to his voice, make eye contact, and stumble across the towel to him. The imprinting continued.

After about six hours, as the first hatchlings dried out, Joe decided to move them to a brooder. This was a box about 24 inches square and 18 inches high with a waterer and a 100-watt lamp to provide heat. Joe added a feeder filled with high-quality poultry feed. The poults also liked to peck at ants and chase any small insects that flew by.

As more and more poults dried out, they were transferred to the brooder. Joe kept his face very close to them, talking often and letting them get familiar with everything about him.

He noticed that they were uncomfortable with anything that passed overhead. He wondered if this could be a built-in warning for eagles, hawks, and other circling predators. He wanted to be able to pick up the poults without stress so he passed his hands back and forth above them until they got used to this action and ignored it.

A poult resting on straw, at one week old.

All were healthy except one that was very weak. This one stayed in the incubator. On Sunday, May 12, the weak turkey died. Joe was upset and thought it might be an unfortunate defect. The others from clutch #2 continued to be strong, active, and vocal. Joe had managed to watch all the poults from clutch #2 hatch and imprint. There were, however, four eggs that still hadn't pipped.

When Joe sat on a cushion and talked with *peeps* and *trills*, the poults came near and stared at his eyes. It was very intense, as if he were the only thing in the room. Some liked to be held and fell asleep in his hand. Others found special places on his shirt, hat, or near his legs where they could snuggle. And a few were shy and did not come so close. He was starting to be able to tell them apart both by their looks—like a crooked toe—and their behavior.

In the brooder box, the warming light attracted insects, and the poults would chase them. The poults weren't very strong yet and sometimes fell down. Once in a while, they managed to catch something, shake it until it was dead, and then gulp it down. Some poults were aggressive and tried to steal. Others were learning good ways to protect what they had. All of them had great trust in Joe, a powerful connection that he felt was so rare and extraordinary. He could see it and feel it in their responses to him. Joe in turn had great respect and admiration for these wild hatchlings.

WHO NEEDS HELP?

LIFE AS A wild turkey parent was getting rich and also very complicated. Always Joe was listening, feeling, and watching carefully to help him understand turkey behavior. Whenever possible, he quickly scribbled thoughts and observations into a daily journal. He wanted to figure out what they already knew. And he also wanted to figure out how much help he, the "mother," should or could provide.

One of the first things Joe noticed, much to his delight, was that the hatchlings could peck. They pecked even before they could walk. They pecked when there was no food. They pecked at dark things sitting on lighter material and light things sitting on dark material. They could see well and aimed their beaks at the object of their curiosity.

So the wild turkeys did not need any chickens around to show them how to peck—this was a myth. He made arrangements to give away his Rhode Island Reds. He was sure that wild turkeys were much smarter than people thought and now he hoped to learn just how smart they really were.

As he watched them explore, sip water, and eat new things, he saw a poult start to jerk and fall over. Joe thought it was probably ill from something it ate. He put it in the incubator and it soon recovered. That was a good way to help.

Joe had worked constantly for 24 hours while the first 10 poults hatched. He was there for the successful imprinting of each one, and now he was exhausted, having had little sleep for two long days.

But he still had worries about clutch #1. Although many had finally pipped, none were breaking out of the shell. Was the humidity wrong? Had they been in the incubator too long?

In the end he decided not to help. Instead he would wait and see what would happen.

CHAPTER 3

Eggsitter, Caregiver, Turkey Walker

THE SECOND HATCHING

ON MONDAY, MAY 13, hatching activity finally began for clutch #1. Joe was already very tired from the 24-hour vigil for clutch #2, but he talked to them with soft encouragement. It was so exciting as they responded with a chorus of turkey talk.

Joe was now focused on being a busy single parent to poults in three stages of development. From dawn to dusk he switched back and forth between them, talking, listening, hoping to be just what they needed as they started their new lives.

As the eggsitter, he kept watch at the incubator so he would be there for each new hatchling to imprint upon.

As the caregiver, he made sure the wet, weak hatchlings were kept warm.

When he could take a break from the other two responsibilities, Joe moved into his new role as a turkey walker. The oldest poults were growing fast, getting restless and ready for action, so he took them outside for the very first time. He carried them in the brooder box, and they focused on his face and listened carefully to his turkey talk.

Once exposed to the warm sunshine they seemed curious but not afraid. For a very long time, they stared at the vast blue sky like it was the most amazing thing they had ever seen.

A TEST OF THE TURKEY TALK

When their behavior returned to normal, Joe carefully put them down in the grass and kept them corralled between his legs. Right away they started to peck and scratch and made no attempt to hide or run away. But was the imprinting strong enough that they would respond to his mothering? He let a few of them explore farther. It was a test. Would they run off or return when he called them?

Joe *yelped*. He was relieved to see all the little poults come running back to him. Once he voiced a high-pitched alarm *putt*, one of many sounds used by a turkey hen. This caused all the little hatchlings to run back in a panic and hide trembling around his legs. He was glad to see this response and knew that he would use it only in the event of extreme danger.

Wild turkeys make many sounds. A high-pitched *kee kee kee*, three syllables and ending with a *yelp*, is one of the first calls learned by the poults. This "lost" call means they are looking for Mother. They also *whistle* when lost or separated. They *yelp* to greet others early in the morning. They *cluck* to get attention. They *cackle* when flying down from a roost. A hen can *hiss* to indicate a danger. The male toms *gobble* to attract a hen and also drum. A soft *purr* means they are contented. The loud, sharp one-syllable alarm *putt* is used when the hen spots danger.

Similar sounds can have different meanings depending on loudness, the number of syllables, body language, who makes the call, and other variables. Joe was constantly adding to his knowledge of turkey talk. He already knew many sounds but could see that this was not enough. More and more communication was going on that was hard to describe. Some of the "talk" was similar to gestures from a human baby—like an unspoken shrug, grimace, or head shake—that parents gradually learn to understand.

MOST HATCH BUT SOME DON'T

AFTER AN HOUR OUTSIDE, the poults were tired and fell asleep in a pile around Joe's folded legs. He brought them back inside and took a look into the incubator. More little poults were hatching and he greeted them all.

The last four eggs from clutch #2 still had not pipped. He decided to take them outside and crack them. They apparently were sterile and had cooked in the incubator; they looked like hard-boiled eggs. With the one that had died, nine hatchlings remained from clutch #2.

But hatching was progressing successfully for clutch #1. There was one sterile egg and one dead egg, but 14 poults hatched over 27½ hours. Joe managed to be there for every single one. As each new turkey imprinted on him, he cuddled and comforted it. They stared at him intensely and simply adored their "mother." Joe felt it was such a powerful and humbling experience to have these wild birds identify him as the most important thing in their world.

While they hatched, Joe continued to communicate with soft encouragement to the older poults in the brooder by his side. It was difficult to take care of all hatchlings, the brooder, and the incubator too. The entire hatching process took almost four days, and during that time he got very little rest and hardly saw any other people. Occasionally he grabbed an apple or cola for a quick snack, but he was looking forward to a warm, leisurely meal with Claudia.

Joe stayed with the poults as much as possible to create an uninterrupted world of wild turkeys and "mother." This was before the time of cell phones, but if he had owned one, he wouldn't have used it except in an emergency.

He did, however, continue to take notes on all turkey behavior. One turkey was already strutting the way an adult gobbler would do, with wings back and tail up. He was also aggressive and curious. Another wanted to be held all the time. Yet another did not want to be touched but stayed close to Joe's feet. He began to notice many different personalities in the flock—or group—of turkeys: curious, smart, aggressive, shy, slow, sleepy, friendly, talkative, and so on.

As additional poults dried off and became restless, Joe wondered if he could safely mix the two clutches in the brooder. The poults from clutch #1 had lighter coloring, with brighter yellow, paler brown, and fewer brown streaks on their heads than those from clutch #2. Joe worried that the older, bigger ones, with varied markings and different sizes, might become bullies to the younger poults. He decided to separate them in the brooder with a towel and clothespins.

The poults, however, ignored their differences and crept under the towel. They made a nice warm bundle and slept together in a comforting pile of fuzzy yellow and brown.

POULT PROBLEMS

ON TUESDAY MORNING, May 14, Joe greeted the poults and noticed one of them stumbling in the brooder. It had "spraddle leg," probably from getting crushed by sleeping at the bottom of the pile. It could barely walk, standing was impossible, and sitting made the condition worse because the extra weight separated its legs. Joe gently held the poult in his hand with its knees apart and feet crossed. After a few minutes of this, the poult could walk better so Joe repeated the stretch of the tendons. After periods of sleep and then more treatments, the little turkey kept on improving.

At another return to the brooder, he found three young ones, just out of the incubator, dangerously wet after falling at the waterer. Two of them were shaky and staggering. The third was down and unable to open its eyes. When Joe warmed them in the incubator, they all recovered well.

Back and forth, looking here and there, Joe was having a hard time keeping up with all the different needs of the poults. He now realized that one of their greatest threats was getting chilled. Even when it was 80°F, these young turkeys could get cold and shivery in the shade or wet grass. On later adventures, he would make sure the dew had evaporated and the sun was shining in places where they might want to go.

He was learning that he needed to pay close attention to every detail. How many problems would he be unable to solve? And what else could he do to protect the poults?

Hatching Success Chart

	Clutch #1	Clutch #2
Clutch size	16	14
Number eggs incubate	15	14
Began incubation	May 3, 1:00 A.M.	May 7, 6:00 P.M.
First hatch	May 13, 8:00 A.M.	May 10, 5:00 P.M.
Last hatch	May 14, 11:30 A.M.	May 11, 5:00 P.M.
Total hours hatching	27 ½	24
Number of sterile eggs	1	4
Number of dead eggs	1	none
Mortality first 24 hours	none	1
Number of hatchlings	14	9
Total	23	

CHAPTER 4

No to Bright Blue and to Some of the Bugs

THE TOWEL EXCHANGE

A BIG PART OF being a turkey parent was keeping things clean. Joe changed soiled towels at the bottom of the brooder three times a day. He hosed them off and then washed and dried them to reduce the chance of infection or disease. He used old towels in faded earth tones of brown and green.

On Wednesday, May 15, he needed clean towels but his supply was still damp in the dryer. He managed to find a clean, dry replacement in the house. It was bright blue. As always he carefully, gently, slipped it under the poults to cover the bottom of the brooder. But this time the turkeys were alarmed! They retreated to the corner with their heads raised on high alert.

Joe wondered if he had made the exchange too quickly. He tried turkey talk and gentle gestures to soothe them. Nothing worked. Finally he replaced the bright blue towel with a pale brown one. All behavior returned to normal.

BUSY GROWING UP

THE NEXT MORNING, Joe returned to the brooder just before sunrise and was greeted as usual by the chattering of little turkeys. They were so happy and relieved to see him. Some were just two days old, but in the older ones Joe observed wings that had grown longer overnight and tail feathers that were poking through fluffy down. They were looking more alert and ready for action. The oldest poults were 4½ inches tall, six days old, and just one day from being ready to fly. Then where would they want to go?

Joe enjoyed sips of hot coffee and lots of turkey talk while watching the growing brood. Sometimes they exchanged intense stares. Once the sun warmed things up, they went outside. Joe sat with them in a wire circle he had made from stiff poultry wire. Immediately they set about pecking, scratching, and investigating this new environment.

As Joe thought about how he could keep them safe, he

envied these moments when they focused on discovery. Sometimes they performed a "happy dance," ducking and dancing around with wings outstretched. Joe often saw this dance when they were over-joyed to greet him.

But mostly the turkeys were busy. One popular activ-ity was stretching out on the ground and basking when-ever they found a

Upright poult at one week.

warm spot of sunlight. Joe saw so much of this sunbath-ing behavior that he wrote into his journal that gather-ing up sunshine, like eating protein, was an important part of their development.

The birds also enjoyed giving themselves dust baths. They scratched a depression into a dusty anthill for this purpose. Then they kicked up dirt and flapped their wings to get it into their feathers. This is a good way for wild turkeys and other birds to keep their feathers clean. The dust particles absorb oil and dry skin and then fall away. The cloud of dust may also smother lice, feather mites, and other parasites.

BIG APPETITES

A LARGE FOCUS of young turkey activity was eating. They needed protein to grow and looked everywhere for it. Joe, as a naturalist, carefully observed and recorded the diet of these young hunter-predators.

They caught flies, ants, gnats, and leafhoppers. They snatched up black field crickets and small grasshoppers and shook them until they were dead. Then they gulped them down. One poult called out with the alarm *putt* when he found an impressively large grasshopper.

Several differences can be seen in these two poults at one week.

Then there was the love bug. Every little turkey that tasted this acidic March fly spat it out immediately. Other creatures that they knew not to eat were completely ignored, like bees, wasps, and any black spittle bugs that had three pink bands. They loved small spiders but bypassed larger ones like the wolf spider. They shook and devoured centipedes but only pecked at— and did not eat—the millipedes. They ate seeds when they found them. And they gulped sand and grit too because they needed these abrasive materials to digest their food.

After an hour of high-level browsing, everyone was exhausted. In the wild, poults would snuggle under the wings and body of the hen. Instead Joe lay on the ground and all the little turkeys slept around his head, chest, shoulders, neck—anywhere they could snuggle. Joe napped too, until one that had been snoozing on his chest pecked him on the lip.

One little turkey, later named Spooky, somehow ended up with a damaged tail. The others tried to peck away the injury but only made it worse. Joe put the turkey into a towel-lined (not bright blue) cardboard box to protect it from the group. The injured poult began a loud and desperate "lost" call—*kee kee kee*—meant to reach a hen who is far away. The flock stayed right by the box to comfort it with turkey talk and Joe spent extra time with it while the injury healed.

THE BIG MOVE

SO FAR IN THIS ADVENTURE, the poults were doing well enough, but the environment on the plantation was not a good place for them to grow up. There was too much noise and dangerous activity, with clankity tractors, rumbling wagons, and clomping mules and horses. Speeding vehicles and barking dogs were around too. There was even a rifle range.

Joe not only wanted to keep his turkeys safe, he wanted to share their lives as they would live in the wild. He wanted to blend in, to be one of the flock. He wanted to see, hear, and smell everything as close as possible to the way wild turkeys experienced the world. To do that, something needed to change.

Joe and his wife, Claudia, owned several acres of an abandoned farm about 40 miles away, next to the Bradwell Bay National Wilderness Area and a stream called Mill Creek that drains out of Apalachicola National Forest. Claudia had named their property the Wren Nest, and they liked to stay at the small cabin when she wasn't teaching. The land consisted of hammocks with hardwood forests surrounded by wetter land including cypress swamps, pine flatwoods, palmettos, tall grasses, and titi trees. It was a quiet place where the turkeys could roam free and grow up without much interference.

On Friday, May 17, Joe made a decision to move the poults to this property. He ordered wood, nails, wire fencing, and other building materials to be delivered to the farm so he could build a roomy and safe pen when they arrived. He also obtained a larger brooder for the growing flock.

Then, in the darkness of night, he quietly loaded up the turkeys and slowly drove them to their new home. In this way, the change was made with as little disturbance as possible.

CHAPTER 5

Welcome to Wren Nest

WIRE WALLS FOR SAFETY

On Saturday, May 18, Joe got right to work on the pen. During five days of construction, the fast-growing poults were kept in the new brooder. It was warm and clean and had more room than the old one. Sometimes they went on nearby adventures with Claudia, who sat outside with them in the portable wire circle. There were new things to investigate, but it was not enough of a distraction. Often they missed Joe, even when they could see him. They cried out with the "lost" call, *kee kee kee*. He spent as much time as possible with them between digging postholes and pounding nails.

Considerable thought went into the construction of

the new home. At 16 feet wide, 24 feet long, and 8 feet high, it was as big as a house and, Joe hoped, a place where they would be protected until they were large enough to be safe from most predators. A neighbor helped install the posts and overhead joists for a strong basic framework. Then Joe dug a trench all around the pen and used his archaeologist training to make it very straight and neat. Poultry wire was fitted into the entire trench.

Tighter wire fencing was then added over the poultry wire, both belowground and to three feet above, and the trench was filled with dirt. The underground wire was meant to keep raccoons, coyotes, dogs, and even bears from digging in. Wire walls would allow for air flow but would discourage bobcats, rodents, possums, and other predators. He covered the entire top with more wire mesh to prevent owls, eagles, and hawks from swooping down. He added a sloping roof over part of the pen as a rain shelter. Had he missed anything?

Joe had lived in the area for more than 20 years and tried to think of every possible danger he might have seen during that time.

The pen needed to be built in a clean area so that bacteria or parasites that might have sickened other poultry in the past could not be passed along to the turkeys. The eggs of one parasite can cause disease even after four years in the soil. Since no domestic poultry had been raised at Wren Nest, this was not a problem.

Pen completed

But there were other wild turkeys around. It was possible that Joe's flock would pick up the fowl pox virus or other illnesses from them. Fowl pox is a worldwide bird illness related to chicken pox. They almost surely would get it at some point. But would they get sick with something more serious? Blackhead disease, for instance, was known to kill entire populations of wild turkeys.

On Thursday, May 23, the pen was completed. In the corners, Joe propped up limbs from sparkleberry trees—a large type of blueberry tree—to provide places where the birds could roost. Now between 9 and 13 days old, the youngest poults had been flying for only about three days. But they could fly up, in, and around the corners without colliding with the wires. They liked to roost on the limbs and study their surroundings from this height.

While the poults adjusted to the new pen, they were not afraid. But they reacted with caution to everything from a red-tailed hawk flying overhead to the tiniest bug on a leaf. Joe found it hard to keep up with all their activity. Since it wouldn't always be warm enough to take them out to browse, he bought live crickets from a bait shop. Every day he added 200 hopping crickets to the food supply to make sure the poults got enough protein. But he had other things to worry about besides food. That afternoon a possum came much too close to the new home. Mother Joe chased it off with a leftover piece of construction wood.

Crickets are a great source of protein.

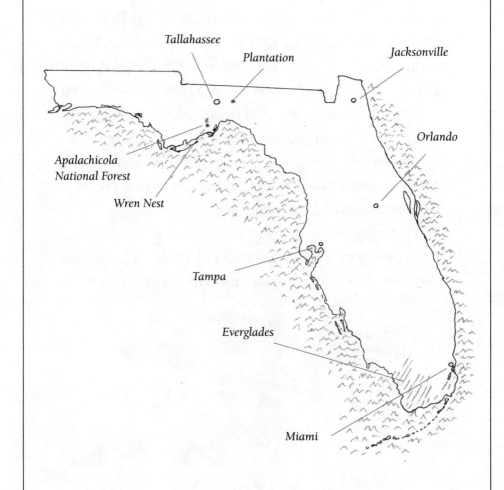

FLORIDA

Tallahassee

Plantation

Jacksonville

Orlando

Apalachicola
National Forest

Wren Nest

Tampa

Everglades

Miami

DANGER LURKS

THE SUN SHONE bright and warm on Friday, May 24, so Joe took everyone outside to the edge of an old field. The cautious turkeys stayed near him at first but soon began to ramble off for short expeditions. Then they dashed quickly back to Joe. Not wanting to interfere with their activities, Joe tried to stay hidden under low pine boughs where he could watch them preen, dust, sleep, and explore. Everywhere there were flurries of yellow flies and mosquitoes. They were a bother to Joe but the poults snapped them up in midair for a quick meal.

Then things went wrong. Joe had dozed off and suddenly awoke to a whooshing flap of wings. A hawk had swooped down and spread its wings over a poult it

Red-tailed hawk

killed. Then it saw Joe, took off quickly, and dropped its victim. The startled little turkeys scattered in every direction. The air rattled with *kee kee kees* and *yelp yelp yelps* until all the poults returned to Joe and he led them back to the pen.

Joe buried the bird so that no wild animal would eat it and get a taste for wild turkey. The little grave was marked with a palmetto leaf. Joe felt sad and embarrassed too. He realized that concealing himself had made it harder to protect these small turkeys.

BECOMING A PROPER TURKEY

ON SUNDAY, MAY 26, there was too much rain to head outside of the pen. Because of the chill, the poults spent time in the brooder, a good place to keep warm but not a good place for growth and development. Finally the sun came out and dried things up. Then they could run around. With all the moisture, deer flies, yellow flies, mosquitoes, and gnats were everywhere. Frogs and toads emerged to eat them and croak and rattle their wonderful songs.

Every day Joe was discovering something new about this flock of turkeys. Something he could hardly miss was their sensitivity to color. They were now involved in Joe's choice of clothing. If he wore a red or purple shirt, they would pull and tug and try to get it off. They didn't like his shoelaces or unfamiliar shoes and boots either.

Frogs help to control flies, mosquitoes, and gnats.

They seemed determined to teach him how to be a proper turkey. Joe decided to wear only faded blue jeans and faded blue T-shirts. Perhaps they liked this color because it was similar to the head of a wild turkey hen.

The poults had strong opinions about Joe's eating habits too. They thought his food must be turkey food and tried to grab it. He could eat around them only by quickly munching on an apple as they walked or maybe sipping some cola or coffee. He ate his main meals when he left them after dark. He did anything and everything he could to encourage the poults to ignore him. He wanted each poult to focus on being a wild young turkey.

At night, when it was dark and they were sleeping, the poults were okay by themselves. All their bodies together made a nice warm biomass and they didn't

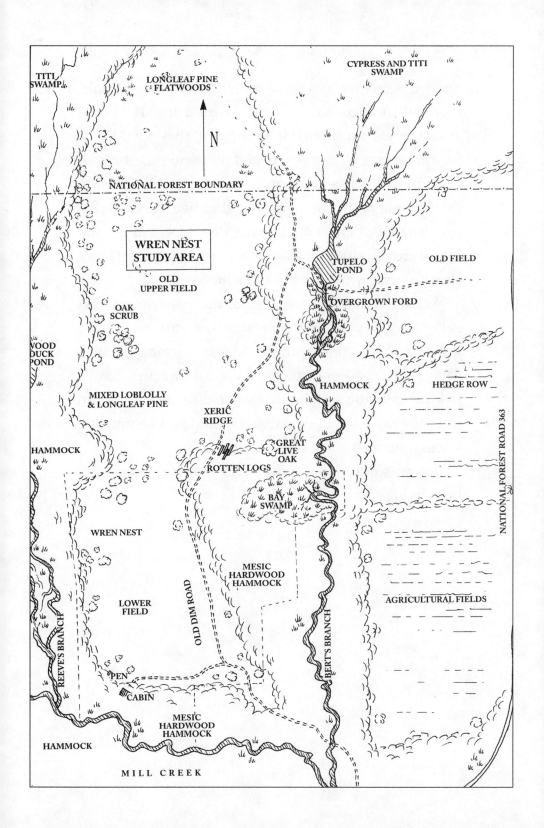

know if a mother was there or not. But in the daytime, they still needed much attention from Joe. If he was absent or even just outside of the pen, they would *peep peep peep*, race up and down, and refuse to eat, drink, or rest until Joe sat with them inside. He hadn't foreseen this amount of involvement, and after two weeks, he felt exhausted. But how could he not do it? Joe and the turkeys were creating an unusual, almost magical, relationship between wild animals and a human.

What started out as a scientific experiment was going way beyond that. Joe was not just measuring inches and counting feathers. He was learning intimate details about turkey behavior. But most amazing, he was talking to young turkeys that wanted to talk to him. In fact they expected it, demanded it, and had so much to say in return.

Joe was entering a wild world that had previously been hidden from view.

CHAPTER 6

Head to Shoulders in Wild Turkeys

STAYING IN THE PEN

On June 1, the three-week-old poults were growing fast. The smallest were six inches high, while the largest had reached eight inches. They had new flight feathers and excellent control over takeoffs and landings. They flapped up to perch on Joe and pushed and shoved to occupy their favorite spots. As they preened to keep their feathers in good shape, Joe was now head to shoulders in wild turkeys.

They had been born knowing certain behaviors, like strutting, pecking, or mild play-fighting. They also would lie down with their necks outstretched to show submission. When they got older, these postures became more common. As both males and females tried out these roles over and over, sometimes they were leaders, at other times they were followers, and sometimes they stayed on the sidelines to avoid the commotion.

Joe was observing all this activity in the pen because he was worried about safety and still hadn't taken the poults anywhere since the hawk incident a week ago. Inside they caught grasshoppers, spiders, and anything with wings that flew through the wire mesh. They would now eat the largest wolf spiders but only after considerable thrashing to make completely sure the spiders were dead. Crickets were big on the menu as were large amounts of turkey starter feed bought in 50-pound bags.

Joe added fresh greens to their diet, like spinach, kale, and the tender leaves of smilax, a vine that he gathered in nearby hammocks. They liked all of the greens until Claudia brought turnip greens still attached to turnips. These were greeted with alarm *putts* and much suspicion. Why? The turnips were bright purple.

It was blackberry season in the flatwoods, and yellow flies appeared everywhere. They had iridescent green eyes and darted about in groups of six or eight. They had a nasty bite and went for Joe and the unfeathered heads and legs of the turkeys. Joe swatted and killed hundreds of them. The poults grabbed them up for extra protein.

SO MANY SNAKES!

MUCH WILDLIFE PASSED by the pen and the curious turkeys watched it all. They saw box turtles and a small chicken turtle. They saw birds like cardinals and jays and reacted to anything that flew overhead. With much better eyesight than Joe, they often spotted things in the sky that he could barely perceive as a tiny speck. As he listened and observed, he was beginning to see and hear the difference in their reaction to a hawk, which would be a predator, and a vulture, which would not.

And then there were the snakes. Some, like a slender black racer and a banded coral snake, slithered in and created a stir as they passed through. The snakes did not seem interested in the young turkeys. The turkeys

The gray rat snake does not have venom.

were curious but did not regard the snakes as a threat. Joe, at this point, did not think snakes would be a problem. Even living many years in the area, he had rarely ever seen them.

One day, noisy young turkeys turned Joe's attention to another visitor. It was a six-foot gray rat snake that had managed to squeeze through the one-inch wire mesh of the wall. Joe made an alarm *putt* to let them know that this was a serious situation. They all came rushing to his side. They uttered confused *putts*, but were not panicked as Joe caught the snake and stashed it in a bag until he could take it to another location.

The next morning, another large gray rat snake slid through and ended up in a bag also. Then an hour later, the poults made the alarm *putt* as another gray rat snake showed up! Joe was astounded to see so many—more in two days than he had seen in years. In other circumstances he might have studied them, but not then. At the first opportunity he whisked them off to other areas of the wilderness.

IT'S A FULL-TIME JOB, MEALS NOT INCLUDED

MEANWHILE JOE CONTINUED to find it hard to enjoy a good meal. The little turkeys were intensely curious about his food and tried to consume anything he had. All these pecking birds made it impossible for him to eat unless it was a quick bite of an apple that he could eat while walking. And if he tried to eat in the house, they made pitiful lost calls whenever he wasn't around. As precocial birds—birds that walk on the first day and gather their own food—they always wanted to follow Mother. Unlike baby hawks and songbirds, which stay alone in the nest, wild turkey poults expect Mother to be with them at all times.

The imprinting with Joe was very strong. He was only able to sneak away in the dark, when they were all asleep and huddled together on a branch for warmth and companionship. If they saw him go, he had to come back and settle them down again. If they flew down to the ground, they were vulnerable to predators.

Still Joe needed food, and spiders and yellow flies wouldn't do. So he continued to eat after he left the poults at night and also used that time to organize his field notes. On rare occasions, he did sneak off for a bite or to run errands.

On Sunday, June 2, when Claudia and relatives were visiting in the house, Joe decided to take a quick lunch break with them. When he heard thunder, he hurried back to the pen to put the poults in the brooder. However, he found them all nervously huddled together in the corner. Another large gray rat snake was nearby and this one had swallowed a young turkey. Now the lump in its body made it too thick to slither back out of the pen.

Joe had thought the poults were too big and too

strong to be eaten by a snake but he was mistaken. They were, however, too big for the brooder. How could he ever leave them alone again?

Feeling sad but determined, Joe quickly set to work building a snakeproof wire box. It was five feet long, three feet wide, and two feet high. The sides and lid were covered with tightly woven hardware cloth, a type of wire mesh that could keep out a large snake. Until the turkeys were old enough to roost outside the pen on high tree limbs, they would now spend their nights safe in this box. Joe put it under the roof with a light and blanket for warmth. He stayed late to make sure they were comfortable.

GROWING UP WILD

THROUGH THIS FIRST MONTH, Joe and the turkeys were really getting to know each other. The poults' extreme curiosity about Joe's behavior was teaching him how to be a proper wild turkey. And Joe was learning how to be sensitive and respond to their expectations.

Meanwhile the poults were growing up just as they should and the largest were already a foot tall. All of them continued to molt new feathers, and for extra protein they ate the small feathers. This loss and regrowth made chilly wet temperatures dangerous for them. They didn't have the right feathers yet to be protected from rain. In their next molt, Joe knew they would start to look more like adult turkeys and would keep those new feathers until the next spring. Much preening and dusting would be needed to keep all feathers in excellent condition.

Wild turkeys are different from domestic turkeys raised on a farm. Wild turkeys are sleek and slim and can fly at 55 miles per hour and run as fast as a man. Domestic turkeys have strong breast muscles, but they are usually too heavy to fly and are poor runners. They grow fast for three months and then they are big enough for the dinner table. Their feathers are usually white. Wild birds have a hard time surviving the first few months of life but eventually have over 5,000 beautiful feathers of red, purple, green, copper, bronze, iridescent gold, brown, and gray. These help them blend into their environment and the lucky ones might survive for several years.

Joe felt like a proud parent as he watched the turkeys grow. As they spent more and more time together, he picked up about 50 sounds of turkey talk and could reproduce them accurately with his voice. Turkey hunters often call wild turkeys by imitating a few of their sounds. Usually they use slate and wood devices or recordings. Joe was interacting with wild birds using a very expanded vocabulary. But something else was happening too. He was learning gestures, shrugs, and other subtle but unspoken ways that the birds used to communicate with him.

The poults listened to every tiny thing Joe said and sometimes had strong reactions. He watched and listened and learned from all their chattering and behavior. He cared about them and didn't repeat things that they found disturbing. Their relationship was becoming a close and unusual bond. He referred to the flock of turkeys as "we" and counted himself as a member. All of them were beginning to experience trust and comfort in the relationship.

Joe was moving deeper and deeper into what he called "my life as a turkey."

This poult at three weeks struts with its tail feathers up, wings dropped low, and head tucked back.

CHAPTER 7

Personality Plus

NOT EVERY TURKEY IS THE SAME

As Joe got to know each poult better, he saw them as separate personalities and gave them names. Turkey Boy was often aggressive and liked to strut from the very first day, but also made friends with a deer. Putt Putt was small and dark. The lower part of her beak, called a mandible, didn't quite fit perfectly with the upper part. Often she wanted to sit in Joe's lap and talk, talk, talk. Little Friend preferred to be at Joe's side, on his lap, or on his shoulder. Sweet Pea settled into his lap whenever he sat and also followed him closely on walks. Bright Eyes had unusually large eyes and a crooked left toe. She

Two-month-old turkeys meeting a deer.

liked to chase friendly squirrels. Because she was the smallest of all, Joe gave her extra crickets.

On Thursday, June 13, when Joe released the turkeys from the snakeproof box, Bright Eyes seemed sluggish and didn't eat her crickets. She didn't eat greens either but did drink some water. Joe wondered if she was getting too chilled at night and watched her closely.

After lunch he decided to release the turkeys from the pen for a short walk. This would be the first time since the incident with the hawk. He wanted to take just five poults as an experiment, but they would only follow him briefly before running back to the flock.

Finally he gave up and took everyone.

THEY DON'T MISS A THING

THE POULTS AND JOE headed for an old field where the turkeys chased after food and investigated longleaf pinecones and everything new. They were cautious but not afraid. It was Joe who carried all the worries and concerns.

Because Joe could not detect things as clearly as they could, the turkeys alerted him to everything of interest. With eyes on the sides of the head and great vision they didn't miss a thing. Here's a snake. It's a rattlesnake. There's a bird. Look, it's a squirrel.

Swallow-tailed kite

And then they waited for Joe to tell them how much danger was involved.

For example, if a hawk flew overhead, Joe would freeze and make a low, cautious *purr*. The turkeys would freeze too, but they remained alert and unafraid. If it was a rabbit, Joe might say, in turkey talk, *Well, that is just a bunny*. Every *yelp* or *purr* from Joe affected their behavior as they froze, scattered, gathered around his feet, or made a thorough investigation in response to "Mother."

Cottontail rabbit

BRIGHT EYES STAGGERS

WHEN THEY RETURNED to the pen after about a two-mile adventure, some of the birds were hot and panting. Bright Eyes was still not eating crickets or greens. The

The poults pointed out everything to Joe: a squirrel in a tree, a snake on the ground, a high-flying hawk almost impossible to see.

next morning she seemed better and ate well, but later Joe saw her stagger and look weak.

On Saturday, June 15, Claudia started up a mower in the distance and the noise made the turkeys jump. Then Joe heard *gobble gobble*, the very first *gobbles* from one of the wild turkeys. The males were now old enough to be called jakes, and their fighting for dominance had become more serious. They clawed with their feet and twisted and pulled the skin of their opponent's head or neck.

In the afternoon, Joe took all the young turkeys on a longer outing. They all stayed very close so he started to worry less about losing any of them.

On Sunday, June 16, Bright Eyes staggered, kicked, and fell backward. It looked like a seizure. Joe picked her up, and she fell asleep briefly in his arms. Then she wanted down, drank some water, and ate crickets. Was she seriously ill or not? Joe was starting to have frustrating dreams at night about wild turkeys, and often he heard "lost" calls, the *kee kee kee yelp*, in his mind.

That night he left the largest turkeys out of the snake-proof cage, hoping that they would roost on the sparkleberry limbs. He got them to fly up but they all fluttered back down and tried to follow him as he walked away. Joe returned after dark and found some of them back on the roosts. The rest he caught and put on the limbs. He now knew that he would have to stay after dark to keep everyone on the roosts overnight.

The next day Bright Eyes had another seizure and

fell over, but again recovered within a few minutes. The other turkeys continued their fast growth. Overnight some of the larger males developed pink areas on their necks where caruncles, fleshy bumps, would eventually hang down. Starker, a large jake with a crooked toe, was the first to have new central tail feathers. As expected, both males and females were starting to get bald spots on their heads. Piles of juvenile flight feathers accumulated on the floor as all molted into new feathers.

Upper Surface of Left Wing

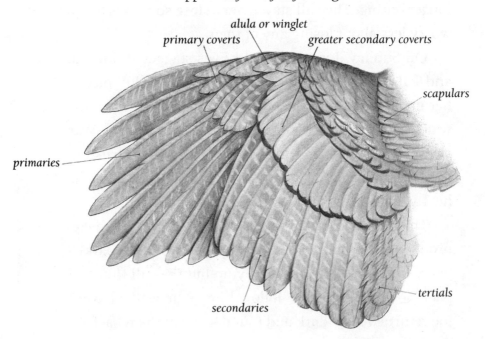

primary coverts   alula or winglet   greater secondary coverts

scapulars

primaries

secondaries   tertials

Joe decided not to take too many notes on the feather changes since this had been well documented by a scientist named Lovett E. Williams Jr. Instead Joe focused on new things they were learning as they adapted to their Wren Nest environment. Would they remember the locations of the best food sources? Would they remember sites where danger had occurred? Would they remember places that they had enjoyed?

TRAGEDY

A HORRIFIC EVENT OCCURRED in the dark of night. Joe didn't hear it. When he returned on Tuesday morning, June 18, he was shocked to discover that a predator had killed three turkeys and eaten their heads. One of the victims was Bright Eyes. Joe was sad that he would never get to know her better. He would miss the way she snoozed on his lap. He would miss caring for her. He thought about wild turkey hens and the terrible obstacles they must face trying to keep young turkeys safe. He wasn't even able to do it with hundreds of dollars' worth of careful construction.

Joe buried the turkeys and then searched the pen for holes or a digging site but couldn't find anything. No snake could have done this. He once heard from a friend that weasels had killed quail in the same manner. He hadn't seen a weasel in over 20 years of living in the area but he set large rat traps outside the pen, hoping to catch one. The next morning the traps were empty and the weasel mystery remained unresolved. Late in the morning, the 18 remaining turkeys took a long, slow walk and all stayed very close to Joe for safety. That night they stayed in their snakeproof/weaselproof cage.

ITCHY ELBOWS AND A SERIOUS COUGH

ON THURSDAY, JUNE 20, the turkeys emerged from the cage in good shape, but Joe had itchy elbows from all the yellow flies. The turkeys could catch them easily and *purr purred* that they tasted good. The jakes were fighting more and some had injuries. They also showed some blue coloring on their heads and the beginnings of dewlaps. The larger jakes were getting especially relaxed with Joe and wanted to sit or sleep in his lap as they had when they were small.

Joe took photos and watched a hen kill and eat a huge centipede. How did she know that its venom wouldn't hurt her? He thought about his respect for all creatures. Every survivor had to eat something.

The turkeys were growing fast and now ranged from 18 to 24 inches, about halfway to their adult height. Every time Joe walked with them, he got more in tune with their world. He learned the location of the cuckoo and kingbird nests in the loblolly pine. He saw a scissortailed flycatcher, the first one he'd spotted in 20 years. When he leaned against a tree to work on his field notes, the turkeys tried to squeeze behind his back or under his knees to hide or warm up. Just as thick, glossy feathers helped them to slither through tall grass, they also helped the birds to snuggle into small warm spaces.

But someone had a cough and it was Putt Putt. She was resting on Joe's lap and breathing through her open bill. On Sunday, June 23, she seemed better and all went for a walk. They foraged mostly under longleaf and lob- lolly pines regrowing in an area that had been cleared of large trees. They stalked flies and gulped some spiders. The turkeys were big enough to eat most grasshoppers but they ignored the Georgia thumper, which can be enor- mous and spits up a foul liquid called tobacco juice when threatened. Putt Putt coughed and gagged but still man- aged to consume a very large katydid.

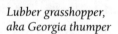

Lubber grasshopper, aka Georgia thumper

MORE TURKEY TALK

JOE WAS LEARNING new turkey talk as he picked up their warnings for various birds and how they were flying. For instance, they reacted differently to a predator hawk than they did to a noisy crow. A nasal *whine* meant "pay attention, but this is not an alarm." A rising *purr* meant "freeze" or "gather together and be still." An alarm *putt* meant "dive for cover under a bush." The type of *purr* varied depending on whether the bird was flying straight toward them or soaring far overhead. A low *hiss* kept everyone silent until the hawk was out of sight and then *trills* and *purrs* resumed as all behavior returned to normal.

As Joe used this new talk, it became strongly reinforced with the turkeys. When they were out on walks, they never saw other humans and Joe rarely used his human voice anymore. When he did, the flock usually ignored him. He once tried to hide from them, but they didn't miss a clue and walked right to his location. Their connection was growing and Joe could see that they were becoming real wild turkeys and not turkeys raised in a pen.

On Tuesday, June 25, Putt Putt fell down on a walk so Joe carried her back to the pen. The next day, he felt sad to leave her behind in the snakeproof/weaselproof cage. The other turkeys came across a rattlesnake, which can inject venom in its bite, and a black racer, a snake that is not venomous. They slowly approached the rattlesnake with cautious *putts* and necks outstretched. They were alarmed, however, when the black racer made a strike at Joe's leg after he stepped on its tail, hoping to scare it away. Joe gave several loud alarm *putts* and they ran to another area. In spite of the irritated black racer, the turkey talk and behavior showed that they had recognized that the rattlesnake was a greater threat.

When the rain started, they returned to the pen. Joe sketched a three-foot plant called penstemon, or beardtongue, which he saw in abundance, while one turkey slept on his shoulder, another sat on his lap, and the rest stayed very close. He learned more turkey talk too. *Shuuck shuuck shuuck*. This was a nasal sound they made as they passed nearby or when he touched them. It was talk just for him and not shared with other turkeys. Joe wasn't sure what it meant but liked to think that it was because they really liked him.

On a rainy day Joe could work on an illustration of penstemon, or beardtongue, even with turkeys climbing all over him.

THE SMALLEST DOESN'T SURVIVE

AS THE DAY CONTINUED, Putt Putt, the smallest, was looking worse and was not interested in food or water. Joe did not see any evidence of fever or infection and thought she probably had a physical problem.

On June 27, Putt Putt died in the night. Sadly, Joe buried her in the turkey cemetery with the others. Of 24 hatchlings, two had been lost to sickness and five to predators. He was determined to keep giving the rest of the wild turkeys the best care he could. But how long would it take? How many would survive? And would they eventually be able to take care of themselves and raise a family?

It was a commitment that he couldn't leave. For eight weeks he had gulped food late at night, slept rarely, scratched itchy elbows, had limited contact with family and friends, and had no financial income.

And yet he was talking to turkeys and they responded to him in incredible ways. He felt unconditional affection for these birds as if they were his own children. They shared a language and unique experiences. He didn't feel superior to or different from them. He was one member of the flock, living a wild, mysterious life through their eyes.

CHAPTER 8

Out of the Cage and Up to the Roost

HOT, HOT, HOT

FRIDAY, JUNE 28, brought a welcome change for the turkeys. After they'd spent 10 nights in the snakeproof/weaselproof cage, Joe decided to let them out. With Putt Putt gone, the six-week-old turkeys were now large enough to stay all night on the roosts. Because they were always safer up on the limbs, Joe assumed the earlier losses were the result of some birds roosting on the ground. During the night, he checked them several times. All remained on high roosts. Joe was feeling a renewed confidence with this group. For the first time, he didn't have any unhealthy or underdeveloped birds.

The next night Joe checked the flock two times. Since

they were doing so well he didn't come back until morning. Saturday, June 29, was a scorcher so they tried an early slow walk. Soon they were racing through the field, side by side, to flush out moths, butterflies, and grasshoppers. It was a good strategy because as the insects tried to escape from one turkey, they often landed right in front of another. After hunting, everyone returned to the pen overheated and panting.

Moth

Spooky, the hen that had once been pecked and then separated from the flock because of an injury, did not eat. She could hardly swallow, her wings were drooping, and she had diarrhea. Spooky was dark and her left middle toe turned inward. Joe watched over her closely. After an hour, she was better and managed to stay up on the roost. Since it was more than 100°F, Joe wondered if she had heatstroke. He decided to keep everyone cool and calm in the shady pen. Joe removed the snakeproof/weaselproof cage, and there was more room for everyone.

As they spent extra quiet time with Joe, some turkeys liked being stroked and even fell asleep. Starker, one of the larger males, wanted to snuggle as close as possible on Joe's lap. But if Joe reached out to touch him, he moved away. He returned to snuggle only when Joe was busy doing something else, like writing in his notebook. Some of the others did this also.

Joe thought about this behavior. Turkeys are birds

that have no means to grasp or hold on to anything, unlike other birds, like raptors, that use their feet to grasp. So when Joe reached out with a hand, the turkeys were uncomfortable. Grasping was not something they did to show affection. It was a behavior they

Wild turkeys can identify different birds from a great distance. This hawk is a raptor.

experienced as the action of a predator. But Joe felt deep affection from them, and for them, in many other ways.

A vulture is a scavenger.

ROTTEN PINE LOGS AND NEW FEATHERS

ON TUESDAY, JULY 2, Joe and the flock took a walk along an old roadbed. They found a circular patch of crushed thick grass as if a small deer had used it for a bed. The turkeys were intently curious but finally left to browse in the blackberries. As they ran to catch up with Joe, there was a loud *buzz* and a *hiss*. A five-foot rattlesnake recoiled near Joe's foot. Joe made the alarm *putt*, and the turkeys flew off to a pile of rotten pine logs, the likely home of the snake. With *yelps* and alarm *putts*, Joe led everyone back to the roadbed.

When they returned to the pen, Joe saw that he had left the door open. Two grackles were inside but the turkeys were not impressed by these black birds. With the lure of Joe's crickets, the turkeys walked right in and the grackles flew out the open door.

The next day, the turkeys had a new appearance again. They looked more like sleek adults, with less down on their heads, longer tails, and powerful legs. The jakes had more swelling in the neck caruncles. While handling a jake, Joe watched a bright red caruncle slowly turn pale. It was the first time he'd observed this ability to change skin color in response to excitement.

Some turkeys now had beautiful purple and bronze iridescent feathers common to all wild turkey adults. In clutch #2, as their yellow down became darker, the turkeys looked blotchy. The lighter ones from clutch #1 molted more cleanly on their heads and had a pale blue appearance that looked much neater. Most had two pairs of central tail feathers and other dark feathers on their backs.

These new feathers were very important. They provided protection from water, so Joe no longer had to worry about the birds getting wet. Plus they knew how to stay dry under the rain shadow of the pines and how to shake water from their feathers.

LESS FIGHTING, MORE INDEPENDENCE

THE TURKEYS WERE FIGHTING less and seemed to have discovered that intense battles were painful and tiring. However, they all took turns being submissive, lying on the ground with necks outstretched and eyes closed. Sometimes even the smallest hen might stand over a big jake and peck him on the head for a brief time.

In the afternoon Joe wrote on his porch and kept an eye on the flock from afar. The turkeys watched him for a while but then went back to normal behavior. They no longer needed him every waking minute. He noticed that sometimes they wanted to be with "Mother" and sometimes with the flock. Lately the stronger urge seemed to be with the flock.

At first he thought perhaps they had not totally imprinted on him. But later he decided that a group offered greater safety as they watched out for each other with constant turkey talk. And if one got separated, it was easier to find the noisy group making lost calls than an individual.

NEW DISCOVERIES

ON SATURDAY, JULY 6, a red-shouldered hawk flew overhead while everyone was in the pen. The turkeys paid little attention, so Joe made a soft alarm *putt*. The birds panicked and hit the fence; one ended up with a minor cut. Joe learned that the turkeys were getting too big and strong to hit the wire so he decided to no longer make alarm sounds inside the pen.

When they looked outside the pen, they saw two antlered deer browsing. Joe delayed their walk to allow the deer to finish eating. Then the turkeys rushed off for more blackberries and deerberries. Three turkeys *putted* to announce they had discovered a broken piece of a wild turkey egg. One took a small bite and Joe picked up the pieces. Farther along, they found another broken egg and a freshly dropped large tail feather from a resident wild turkey. All were impressed and gathered around for a long look. Would they ever have such amazing feathers? And would they ever see these resident wild turkeys up close?

A SNAKEY PLAN

ON SUNDAY, JULY 7, Joe returned by himself to the pile of rotten pine logs. He wanted to see if the big rattlesnake lived there. He poked and prodded, and found it hidden in a damp log shaded by deerberry, wild azalea, and grasses. As it slithered away, he counted 13 rattles. This large poisonous snake was too dangerous to have nearby and he would have to do something about moving it.

Years earlier, when he had worked for a zoo and handled snakes, he used a snake hook and other tools to handle the animals safely. So far Joe had been lucky and had never been bitten. But now he had only a hoe and shovel. Would this be enough? He began to think of a good plan that would be safe for him and safe for the snake too.

LITTLE FRIEND

ON MONDAY, JULY 8, Little Friend was very sick. He wanted to stand rather than sit and Joe knew this was not a good sign. Had he caught something from the resident wild turkeys? Fowl pox was a sickness that almost all would get, like a human child getting chicken pox. A turkey would get sores on its nonfeathered parts that would grow to look like warts, then scab up and fall off. The pox would usually clear up in two weeks, but what if it was something worse?

When they took a walk, Joe had to leave Little Friend behind in the snakeproof/weaselproof cage. The others had a wonderful day of discovery in new territory. They spotted a quail and many signs of deer. They also spotted a dead gopher tortoise, a reptile that digs out long burrows that are important to many creatures in this environment. They ate persimmon, sparkleberry, deerberry, and gallberry. Joe ate berries with the turkeys but did

Exploring with the brood

not eat any bugs. When a red-tailed hawk landed, Joe stood up quickly and scared it off.

When everyone was suffering from the intense heat, Joe led them to a creek called Bert's Branch. It flowed out of a swampy area into a stream. The water was clear and only a few inches deep. The turkeys were mesmerized by their first look at running water. Some were brave enough to take a sip. There were *yelps* and *putts* as they discovered mushrooms, damselflies, and leopard frogs. When a thunderstorm clashed, they had to leave this astonishing new place and rush back home. Joe wondered: Would they remember this spot in any special way?

At home, they found Little Friend looking worse than before and Joe kept him separated in the cage. His coordination was not good, his head drooped, and his eyes looked peculiar. Joe suspected he might have an infection.

On Wednesday, July 10, Joe added an antibiotic called Terramycin to Little Friend's water. Over the phone a veterinarian friend advised him to give the medicine to all of them, so Joe went into town for more. When he returned, he saw that Little Friend had died. All were sad. Joe added Little Friend to the turkey cemetery.

He was now a parent to 15 wild turkeys. He started them on the medication, one tablespoon in a gallon of water. Only Spooky looked weak. When he handled her, she seemed quite irritated, as though she thought her ill health was his fault.

REMEMBERING THE CREEK

THURSDAY, JULY 11, was equally hot and humid, but all were eager to go out. Eventually they returned to Bert's Branch. The turkeys raced ahead, as they clearly remembered this creek. With no hesitation, they all waded in and drank deeply. In this hardwood area of oaks, they found many things to add to their diet. One turkey plucked a large green anole from a deerberry bush, shook it, kept it away from a jealous rival, and then finally swallowed it. Joe was amazed at their lack of caution. Had they eaten lizards before and he just didn't see it? How did they know lizards were edible?

When they came to a large oak tree, Joe climbed up into the high branches. All the turkeys flew up around him and peered down at the world from this new perspective. When a raccoon tried to join them, there were a lot of *putts* and *jeers* until they chased it off. Then they returned to their behavior of quiet tree sitting.

The next day they found broken turkey eggs in several places but never a nest. The turkeys ate all the eggshells, probably a good source of calcium. Joe felt like they were being stealthily watched by resident wild

The turkeys refused to share their
quiet tree-sitting with a raccoon.

turkeys lurking just out of sight. Would the two groups ever meet?

On Saturday, July 13, the turkeys continued to look healthy and handsome so Joe stopped the medication. Spooky still seemed a bit odd but Joe thought perhaps it was the best she could do. She was friendly once again. She seemed to have forgiven him for her sickness.

They returned to Bert's Branch and this time they discovered the overhanging limbs above the creek. They flew up to admire the view and then moved on to a new spot. They wanted to do nothing more than sit and lounge and stretch. It was their favorite spot. Since Joe would distract them if he pulled any food from his backpack, he quietly ate berries, avoided the bugs, and thought about a good plan to deal with the rattlesnake.

The next day Joe wore a light brown shirt. He thought the turkeys wouldn't mind, but they disagreed and tried to peck it off. So he went back to wearing his uniform of light blue. When they took a walk in the late afternoon, they saw a deer staring at them. A turkey gave the alarm *putt*, but the doe walked closer, and the turkeys, especially Turkey Boy, quickly decided that this creature could be a friend. Even though it had many features of a coyote, like big ears, a brown furry body, and a long face, they did not see the deer as a threat. It was something they knew without being taught—instinctual information in them since birth. Later, however, they were very disturbed by an elderly box turtle. Joe thought maybe they saw it as a snake in a box.

The grasshoppers were plentiful and did not fly well after all the rain. The turkeys caught them easily until they heard the clapping of another thunderstorm. When they returned to the pen, they gathered around Joe. Sweet Pea, who was always so close, was the first to plop into his lap.

As Joe wrote down his latest observations he realized that there was more going on in every instance,

American bird grasshopper

every encounter, than he could possibly follow or understand. He'd thought things would get simpler as he joined
the flock, but they were getting more complex. He was
beginning to suspect that these fascinating wild turkeys
would always remain a mystery to him.

On Monday, July 15, they returned to Bert's Branch.
The turkeys waded through the plants at the edge of the
water but the mosquitoes were terrible and Joe had to
leave the creek bed. The turkeys flew up near him in the
branches above the creek. Nearby, angry jays and a pair
of crested flycatchers were harassing a red-shouldered
hawk. As yet another thunderstorm approached, they
headed back to the pen. Joe was out of crickets, which he
sometimes used to lure them back in. However, the flock
still chose to follow him.

SNAKE REMOVAL

ON WEDNESDAY, JULY 17, Joe executed his plan to remove the rattlesnake. He carefully searched through the pile of rotten pine logs and finally found it. Then *swoosh!* He lifted it with a garden hoe and quickly lowered it into an ice chest. He worked so fast that the snake had no time to rattle its tail until after he closed the lid. Later he transported it to a remote spot in the forest. As always, he was looking for the best ways to keep his family and the flock as safe as possible.

On their next outing, the fruit-loving turkeys ate some of the very last of the blackberries. What would they eat now? Joe saw different species of grasses drooping with heavy heads. Would grass seeds become the next new food source?

As blackberries and other foods disappeared, the turkeys had to find other things to eat.

CHAPTER 9

Survival and Beyond

SLEEPING IN

THURSDAY, JULY 18, was the third day of heavy rain. Usually Joe never got more than four or five hours of sleep, but with the flock older and more independent, he decided to stay in bed. The turkeys remained on the roost. For the first time all summer there were no gnats. When the rain stopped at 9:00 A.M., it was a delightful morning and Joe thought the turkeys were probably hungry for sun basking and dust baths.

A rabbit sitting under rabbit bells.

When they finally took a walk, the turkeys snapped up seeds and the green pods of a creeping plant called rabbit bells. Some species of the plant are poisonous to livestock, but these pods tasted like English peas. The wild turkeys loved them, and Joe nibbled too. As always when he took a walk with the flock, they didn't come across another human. It was Joe experiencing life as a turkey and turkeys growing up with an unusual mother.

Later Joe watched them fly up to limbs, sit and preen, and then fly off to other limbs to repeat this practice over and over. It involved much noisy flapping and turkey talk. Joe called this "limbing behavior." He had watched it several times before but couldn't quite figure out its purpose. Did it have a meaning beyond survival? Was it playful? Fun?

EXPLORING

THE TURKEYS *putt putted* when they found a small scarlet snake to examine. With red, black, and white bands, it resembled a coral snake but it was not poisonous. Always on walks they were attracted to things that were unusual or different that had nothing to do with their survival. They pointed out old glass, ceramics, lead and brass ammunition, pottery shards from ancient times, flint, old nails, tacks, rusty cans, Day-Glo tape, buttons, and bottle caps. They carried these items around in their bills, and eventually all of the flock would study them.

Bones were of particular interest. When they first found

a bone, they used caution, but then they never tired of revisiting the place to study it again and again. Sometimes they would eat a small chip, but they were also interested in the shape and texture of

Possum skull

the bone. One time a hen carried around the skull of a possum. When she finally dropped it, it became a play object for all the others.

They couldn't pass up feathers and knew the difference between their own feathers and those of other wild turkeys. There were fights and footraces for all small feathers, which were immediately eaten for nutrition. They could tell the difference between weathered tree stumps and ones that had been cut down with a saw. They were interested in all of them but were disturbed and concerned by those cut down with a saw. They also stopped for any new branch that fell from a tree. They approached slowly, heads outstretched, cautious until they had a chance to check it out.

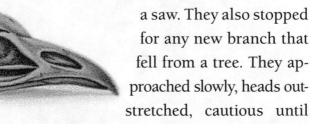

Bird skull

If Joe found something of interest, they all gathered around quietly to observe. When he was done, they would peck and tap to gather their own information.

If Joe pointed at a spider or something they had missed, they would not stare at his finger but would quickly find the object. This is a difficult behavior even for dogs.

Since Joe had always liked to identify plants, insects, bones, reptiles, mammals, and artifacts, he felt like he was in the best company possible. He was exploring with a flock of feathered scientists that had identical interests. Their similarities were greater than their differences.

As they continued on their walk, they came across a large gray rat snake; Joe stayed back to let them examine it on their own. Then, at the creek, he watched a turkey capture, kill, and eat a small frog with an X on its back. It was a spring peeper. Impressive! Now frogs were on the menu.

Later they crossed paths with another rattlesnake. This time the turkeys were nervous and disturbed. They made a staccato *thump thump* with their feet, yet another new behavior for Joe to record in his notes. Each *thump* lasted for only a second or two and then was repeated by a different turkey. They stayed back and were too nimble to get hurt by this snake.

OVERREACTING

ON SATURDAY, JULY 20, they saw a coyote that they had seen before in the distance. Generally quite composed in the face of danger, the turkeys flew up into the trees in a panic with loud *jeers* and *putts*. The coyote was small with very small footprints. Joe was able to track it easily and knew that it had come near the cabin but never near the pen. Joe wondered why the turkeys might be so alarmed by this creature skulking nervously past with its head and tail down. Were they wasting energy by overreacting?

But then he thought about how things might have been a few hundred years ago, even a few thousand—not much time in their history of 20 million years. In ancient times, turkeys lived in Florida with the panther, black wolf, saber-toothed tiger, a type of giant lion, the great dire wolf, and other large predators. Turkeys made a good meal. To survive they needed behaviors to keep ahead of these animals. Even though most of the ancient predators were now extinct, the behavior remained. Joe called this "fossil behavior," retaining a response to a predator that no longer exists. When humans lived in caves, spiders and snakes were a much bigger threat than they are today. Yet some people are alarmed by photos or even the idea of spiders and snakes, which is a similar overreaction.

MORE EXPLORING AND MORE SNAKES

LATER JOE AND THE FLOCK returned to their favorite place, Bert's Branch. This time their attention was caught by the shimmering light reflecting off the creek and onto the underside of the branches. It was glimmering and sparkling like a living, moving thing. The turkeys were enchanted and watched for a long time. Joe sat quietly, trying to be invisible, and enjoying it all. When a wild turkey came to sit on his lap, he felt honored that perhaps she thought he belonged to this incredible natural moment.

On Sunday, July 21, Claudia's family came to visit. The turkeys responded to the varied colors of their clothing with loud *yelps* and *gobbles*. With lots of rain and warm temperatures, the snakes were very active. Two venomous snakes came too close to the pen and cabin. For everyone's safety, Joe carefully removed a 5-foot diamondback rattler and a 30-inch cottonmouth moccasin.

The next day Paw Paw looked sick, tucking her head and sleeping constantly. Joe gave her some medication and she went on the walk. For the first time Joe took a high-resolution video camera to record turkey behavior. He had been reluctant to do this because a camera was not part of the natural world. The turkeys were curious, but he did manage to get shots of them stripping seeds and eating deerberries before the battery gave out after 20 minutes.

Later they found fresh gopher tortoise burrows. When a tortoise digs out a burrow and piles up dirt at the front, this becomes a great place for a dust bath. All the turkeys enjoyed kicking dust into their new feathers to keep them clean.

Relaxing with the young poults.

Turkey Boy at three weeks.

Turkey Boy at two months.

Young turkey alert to possible danger.

Morning nap time.

Sleepy poult.

Starker hunting for grasshoppers.

Bert's Branch.

Turkey Boy as an adult gobbler.

Joe and Turkey Boy.

The pen.

Turkey expedition.

Young turkeys sunning and dusting.

An afternoon recess in the trees.

Rosey trying to be the boss at one year old.

Wild turkeys—always alert.

Sweet Pea—her vision of the world.

Joe and Turkey Boy.

Joe with Button, the fox squirrel he raised from birth.

One of Joe's paintings: Sunrise in the Flatwoods with the Turkeys

Joe and Turkey Boy sharing a few minutes together.

Communicating with Starker.

Taking notice of something unusual.

A special moment with Starker.

Stretch in need of a little affection.

Communicating with Turkey Boy.

Looking at a curious bug with some of the "boys."

Paying close attention to wild-turkey behavior.

Joe and Turkey Boy out for a walk.

Samara flying to join Joe in the old field.

Rosey.

Turkey Boy with the wild flock—the last time Joe saw him.

On the way back, Joe carefully passed the pile of rotten pine logs. Nothing. The place seemed deserted. Then he heard alarm *putts* from the turkeys. There was another rattlesnake. Joe had missed it, but they did not. Because the turkeys were extra curious, Joe tried to move them away with an alarm *putt*. However, they continued to crane their necks and make loud *putts*. Suddenly the snake made a strike and then leaped for the cover of the logs. The turkeys exploded into a loud flight. A couple of them grazed Joe as they sped through the air.

FOWL POX OR GNATS?

WHEN THEY FINALLY returned home, Joe noticed that some of the turkeys had sores on their heads. He thought this might be the first sign of fowl pox. Or was it those gnats?

The next day, Tuesday, July 23, was a scorcher. At 110°F, it was almost too hot to move. Joe, however, needed to open another 50-pound bag of turkey feed because they were eating so much. Paw Paw, who had been feeling ill, looked much better so Joe stopped the medication.

Then he turned his attention to the gnats. All biting insects were in abundance—this was the worst year he had ever seen—but he was especially astounded by the obnoxious numbers of gnats. His face, elbows, and hands itched and burned from the bugs' tormenting bites. They constantly swarmed near his eyes and ears. The turkeys were also annoyed and the sores on their heads seemed to be the result of these pesky insects. They often rubbed their heads on their backs.

Joe collected gnat samples and sent them to the Insect ID Lab at the University of Florida for identification. They called it the "turkey gnat" and said it was the turkey pox vector, able to transmit this disease with its bite. There was no chemical that could control it.

NATURE SCHOOL

ON WEDNESDAY, JULY 24, the turkeys scratched out an arrowhead at the bottom of Bert's Branch. It was a pinkish white flint, sharp and nicely chipped. Joe identified it as from the Savannah River tradition of hunter-gatherers from 4,000 to 6,000 years ago. When he had earlier studied their trash piles as an archaeologist, he found deer, bear, raccoon, and fish remains. But the most common bones found came from *Maleagris gallopavo*, the wild turkey. Sometimes arrowheads were made from the sharp spurs of the gobblers.

Arrowhead

On Saturday, July 27, the turkeys reinvestigated the pile of rotten pine logs. They had a specific memory of that place and always stopped to look closely. This time

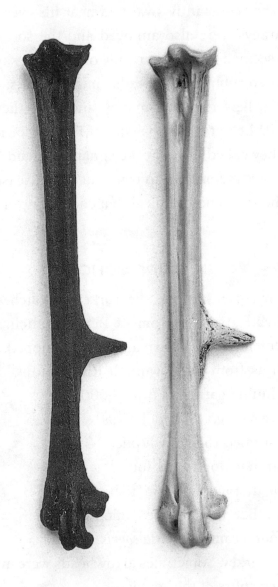

Two lower leg bones from wild turkey gobblers. The one on the left comes from an ancient time when horses, bison, giant sloths, mammoths, and mastodons lived in Florida. The protruding bones in the middle are the sharp spurs.

they discovered yet another rattler. Joe used his video camera to record their craning necks and turkey talk. At first he had been worried about their interest in snakes, but now he realized that ignorance had no survival value. They were highly motivated students that always wanted to learn. If they suspected that something was hiding in the bushes, like a box turtle under a deerberry bush, they didn't stop until they figured it out.

This nature school was always in session, so what would they learn next?

CHAPTER 10

The Joy of New Discoveries

CHECKING THE EDGES

As THE TURKEYS got bigger and stronger, they could take walks of five miles or more. If the weather was good, they might be out for the entire day. But on Sunday, July 28, it was hot and humid. Turkey Boy walked around with one eye closed. Joe thought it was possibly from an injury and watched his favorite jake carefully. Later both eyes were open again as the problem resolved on its own.

They finally got out for a walk at three in the afternoon and headed for an area that had more than one type of environment. It was between Bert's Branch and the east side of an old field. One section was a forest of

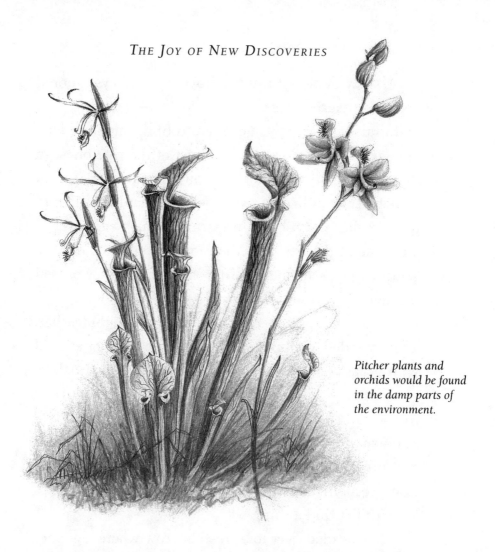

Pitcher plants and orchids would be found in the damp parts of the environment.

longleaf pines. Another area was covered with lichens. Another had oak and other hardwood trees. Above and below that were two swamps. One had wild azalea and gallberry; the other had titi and viburnum.

In mixed areas like these, the turkeys had a greater chance to find something new and interesting. When more than one type of environment meets another, it is called the "edge effect."

As they explored this territory, the turkeys ignored common deerberries and looked for something new and unusual. They were excited to find some rare late-blooming blueberries and ate most of the ripe ones. In their usual manner, they didn't pull unripe berries from a bush. They didn't eat overripe ones that had fallen to the ground. And they didn't strip the bush either. They ate some of the best and then moved on. They did the same with grasshoppers, eating only some as they passed through.

Later they spotted a fresh wild turkey flight feather. They startled, stopped abruptly, and then chattered with great concern that it was not from their flock. It was from the group of resident wild turkeys that lurked in the far edges. Joe wondered how they knew this. They soon passed an area where these resident wild turkeys had scratched for seeds or insects. Joe's flock again recognized the signs and stopped to scratch too. They didn't find a thing.

They headed over to a fresh burrow where a gopher tortoise had been digging a tunnel. They checked for furry wolf spiders, which liked to hide near the opening. Then they used the loose dirt piled up at the entrance for their dust baths. They were not interested in the shed rattlesnake skin that Joe found. But later they were quite excited to point out a box turtle hiding under a small plant called bog button.

Box turtle under bog buttons

SOME ADVENTURES ARE HO-HUM

ON MONDAY, JULY 29, a large pine limb broke and fell beside the turkey pen. The turkeys were alarmed and crashed into the wires. Some ended up with cuts but none were seriously injured. All were able to go on a walk.

The flock spotted a black racer snake, but only about half of them stopped to examine it. Ho-hum. Apparently they had learned enough about it and were no longer impressed. Often now when they found something old and familiar, it got little attention. Instead they hurried past to enjoy the wonder of finding something new.

When they got hungry, they filled up on deerberries and grasshoppers and then sat with Joe under a big pine tree. He heard the *peter peter peter* voice of a little gray bird called a tufted titmouse. During his animal studies, Joe had learned to speak "titmouse," so he answered: *Peter peter peter, tiska say-say.* The turkeys were very confused. *Peter peter peter?* What's going on? Don't say that. As usual, whenever Joe did not use proper behavior, they startled and *tsk-tsked* to correct him. So Joe went back to turkey talk.

Tufted titmouse

Later they found a flight feather from a red-shouldered hawk. The design was similar to a wild turkey feather but they knew the difference. Only two examined it; one pecked at it and then they walked on. Ho-hum. They were not impressed.

This reaction was much more subdued than all the chattering, poking, and pecking they engaged in whenever they found a feather from a resident wild turkey. Their curiosity was simply not satisfied. Joe hoped they would eventually have a personal encounter with other turkeys. Was his presence keeping them away?

Wednesday, July 31, was a pleasant day with a cool wind. The turkeys were excited about the nice weather. Joe sipped coffee, then put a new battery in his video camera, and off they went to sit for hours under the limbs of longleaf pines. Everyone was just glad to be there. The wet grasshoppers were poor flyers and easy to capture. The turkeys pulled and tugged at Joe until he participated in the blackberry feast. All of them ended up with purple mouths.

Later they alerted Joe to a pine bough. A pine bough? He lifted it up and they all took a curious look at a tiny cottontail rabbit with huge black eyes. Their talk and behavior were very different from that used around a rattlesnake. Joe was learning new turkey talk and other ways that turkeys communicated all the time. Some of it seemed so intangible, like electricity snapping through air, that he was finding it hard to put into words.

The turkeys talked and behaved differently around a cottontail rabbit.

Once more they made a visit to Bert's Branch to stretch and preen. They expressed their enjoyment with faint *purr purr purrs*. Joe called this behavior "nooning." The turkeys refreshed themselves at this natural spa, resting in the sunlight and enjoying all the birdsong—except for the hawk, who still inspired an alert.

SNAKES GALORE

LATER THEY RETURNED to the pile of rotten pine logs. Joe videotaped them as they made a quiet approach. Then a turkey made an alarm *putt*. Right in front of Joe's feet was yet another four-foot rattlesnake. Joe leaped away. How had he missed it? They all took a good look and then moved on to study a large coach whip, a fast, non-venomous snake. But when they saw a pygmy rattler, it was ho-hum.

When they returned to the pen, Joe stayed outside to videotape. He was amazed to see the flock choose to go inside without any encouragement from him.

CHAPTER 11

Part Wood, Part Mulch, and Part Feathers

RELAXING IN THE WILD

THURSDAY, AUGUST 1, was a beautiful day, and after browsing they headed back to Bert's Branch. This time Joe was the first to spot a pygmy rattlesnake but the turkeys were again not interested.

Joe was amazed at how many snakes they kept seeing—sometimes four or more in a day. On his own, he might see two in a whole year. Were his human traits not a concern to wildlife now that he was accepted by the turkeys?

The turkeys were 11 weeks old and they wanted to investigate new food sources. Joe watched them add butterfly larvae to their diet of smilax tips, insects,

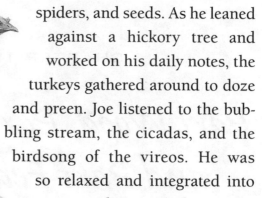

Poult at 10 weeks

spiders, and seeds. As he leaned against a hickory tree and worked on his daily notes, the turkeys gathered around to doze and preen. Joe listened to the bubbling stream, the cicadas, and the birdsong of the vireos. He was so relaxed and integrated into this natural environment that he recorded in his journal that he felt part wood, part mulch, and part feathers. Joe had become so connected to the birds that he often thought of them as "we" rather than "they."

Their rest was interrupted by the appearance of a gray fox that hopped across a log on the other side of the branch. The turkeys jumped to their feet in alert, but Joe remained calm; he felt like he was seeing a lost friend. He had imprinted with and raised a fox from this area that would touch her cool, moist nose to his face as he tried to sleep and sometimes tugged at his hand with sharp teeth. That fox had stayed in his life for a year or two. But this fox took one look at the flock, twitched a bushy tail, and moved quickly on down the creek.

As they returned to the old field, Joe could see that the turkeys were now so large and strong that they were almost the size of an adult turkey in the wild. The males

Gray fox

were the biggest, with some over 40 inches tall, higher than a kitchen counter. Their legs had grown long and powerful and their juvenile feathers had been replaced. Bone and cartilage had developed over their eyes, which gave them the fierce look of a predator. The graceful hen Joe had named Samara was the best at keeping her tail feathers in perfect condition. All the turkeys looked good and were doing just what they should be doing. Joe was a very proud parent.

SNAKE AND GNAT PROTECTION

ON SATURDAY, AUGUST 3, for the first time that summer, Joe wore a long-sleeve shirt in an effort to protect his sore, itchy elbows from more painful insect bites. He also started wearing boots to reduce the risk of a snake-bite. Would they continue to encounter so many snakes?

They did. When they took their walk, the turkeys soon saw their first red rat snake. This species has no venom or fangs but kills by constriction. It is also a very

Damselfly and orchids

good climber. This one did not want to be examined and was outraged by the intense scrutiny of so many large birds. It coiled up and spread its head wide in an impressive threat. The turkeys agreed with Joe's advice to use caution, so they slowly walked away.

Later they ate a few blackberries and then enjoyed a long stay at Bert's Branch. The turkeys stood on one foot, stretched, and made contented *purrs*. Joe was content too. They were enchanted by the dancing crane flies, the whirligig beetles, and the flashing green damselflies that ate gnats. Then thunder cracked as a storm rolled in. Joe quickly covered his video camera in plastic and they hurried back in a downpour. Joe saw yet another rattler in the pile of rotten logs but the turkeys hustled past too quickly to notice.

Sunday, August 4, was still rainy so Joe busied himself with chores. As he and Claudia were covering the garden tractor, lightning struck a tree very near the pen. The turkeys jumped but did not panic. These bright flashes were not new to them. The flatwoods have a long history of lightning that causes a fire now and then and helps to shape the environment.

The rain was just a drizzle in the afternoon so they finally took a walk. The turkeys added tree frogs to their diet along with plenty of larval butterflies, grasshoppers, spiders, and insects. Sometimes they did their "happy dance," jumping, leaping, just having a joyful time.

MEETING MORE BIRDS

THE NEXT DAY was hot and muggy and they found themselves in a mixed flock of noisy birds all darting in and out to gobble up seeds, pound out insects, and snatch up gnats. It was by far the largest gathering Joe had ever seen. There were chickadees and titmice, cardinals and blue jays, wrens and flycatchers, vireos and woodpeckers, gnatcatchers and towhees, catbirds and phoebes, and plenty of warblers. There were even some species that Joe could not identify. The turkeys stopped all activity to stare in amazement. They added *putts*, *clucks*, and *yelps* to the commotion until it all ended after about 30 minutes.

Blue jay

Chickadee

On the way back, they looked for deerberries, but this fruit was getting very scarce. They spotted another black racer and examined it closely. The snake got so angry that it made two lashing strikes at a curious turkey. The bird had no trouble jumping back safely.

That night Joe bought another 50 pounds of turkey feed. He also bought some lightweight mesh camouflage clothing. They were now seeing wild resident turkeys at a distance, and he hoped to become more invisible so the two groups might interact. The turkeys were only mildly accepting of his camouflage and pecked at it now and then in an effort to remove it.

Hatching cicada (molting)

USING THE YELPER

ON WEDNESDAY, AUGUST 7, it was so hot they started a walk before sunrise. As part of his "meet wild resident turkeys" plan, Joe packed his old slate turkey caller, the yelper. It was a handheld device he could scratch to imitate turkey talk. He could make all the calls with his mouth, but his voice did not carry very far. The scratched slate turkey caller would be louder and might get a good response.

In the old field, Joe watched a turkey catch and eat a large buzzing cicada, a rare and special treat. As they headed toward Bert's Branch, they saw two black racers, a gray rat snake, and two box turtles. Then the turkeys *putt putted* to let Joe know that he had walked past yet another rattler. He videotaped their response and then made an alarm *putt* and a *yelp* for assembly. When they sat to rest, some of the turkeys helped Joe eat his apple while others enjoyed blueberries.

Later he got out the slate turkey caller. With it, he made a soft *pit pit* and then a very loud *yelp*. All the turkeys paid attention to the noise, but they did not look at Joe. They stared far off into the woods. In aggressive moods, one jake after another changed color as the sides of their faces turned bright red. Rosey, the one surviving male from clutch #1, had the brightest caruncles of all. Joe stopped using the caller, and after a while, their pale pink color returned.

Besides Rosey, who was the most dominant, only three other jakes remained. These were Starker, Stretch, and Turkey Boy. Almost three months old, they were just beginning to show more aggressive behavior when out on a walk. Fighting and submissive behavior occurred among both jakes and the young hens. Strutting behavior was done by all, but only in the pen.

As a matter of good luck, 11 hens survived in the remaining flock of 15.

As a matter of poor luck, Joe got too close to a saddleback caterpillar with venomous spines. Now his poor elbow was irritated more than ever.

CHAPTER 12

Fly, Fly Away

OUTSTANDING HUNTERS

ON A HOT, hot Thursday, August 8, the flock took their walk early before the dew could evaporate. Joe suffered from itchy elbows, and the turkeys had wet feet and tails. They carefully passed the pile of rotten logs, expecting to see a rattlesnake. But they didn't.

Twenty feet later, they sent a six-foot coach whip, a snake that loves hot weather, into a panic. It started to leap and dart between them. Its home, a rotted-out stump, was surrounded. Which way should it go? Finally it dove into the dark cavity of the dead tree trunk and disappeared. The turkeys looked briefly into the damp hole but it all seemed like too much excitement so early in the morning.

Soon they were eating deerberries and grasshoppers and then foraging at Bert's Branch. They ate smilax tips and spent much time scratching into the leaf litter to find butterfly and moth pupae. They stripped seeds from the grass stems and gobbled down fox grapes. They caught insects so quickly that Joe found it difficult to see and identify everything they snatched.

All in all, they were outstanding hunters. The turkeys ate earthworms and grasshoppers, crickets and katy-dids, cicadas and centipedes, and all kinds of spiders, the bigger the better. They gulped down caterpillars, as well as moth and butterfly larvae (although they ignored the furriest ones), and caught lizards, including green anoles and ground skinks. And then there were the amphibians: bronze frogs, spring peepers, pinewoods tree frogs, squirrel tree frogs, and green tree frogs. They ate all beetles except dung beetles. Sometimes they grabbed up small butter-flies and moths, especially the sulphurs, yellow butterflies with a very long tongue. And they ate large numbers of golden orb spiders, also known as banana spiders.

Pinewoods tree frog

Golden orb spider, aka banana spider

Friday, August 9, was a hot day of similar activity. There weren't too many mosquitoes, and they got relief from the gnats when they returned to the creek. Joe watched a hen stalking a leopard frog in the style of a cat but she was not successful. All the turkeys were very alert to predators flying overhead and Joe assumed that a hawk or owl had recently come close to the pen.

It was miserably hot as they walked back. They found more adult turkey feathers that Joe added to his growing collection. Later he spent time with the turkeys in the pen. Soon his clothes were dirty from muddy feet standing all over him.

NEW BEHAVIORS

As DARKNESS FELL, Joe stood up in the shoulder-high roosting limbs. The turkeys all snuggled up close. They were too big to sit on his head and shoulders but they didn't know it. Joe got a bad scratch on his face when a hen slipped and then tried to climb back up.

Behaviors were changing. The turkeys were growing, and when Joe snuck off for bed, he was sorry that he couldn't stay all night. He was fascinated by how much he could understand of what they wanted to communicate, including nods and shakes and other gestures that had no words.

But Joe could also see that they were maturing. Soon they would be independent. How much time did he have left to be so close? Sometimes when they went out for walks, the birds would fly ahead. At other times they stayed behind and then flew to catch up. These young birds really liked to fly. They had just the right body weight, feathers, and youthful energy to fly often, more than the heavier adult turkeys.

On Saturday, August 10, several turkeys flew out in a wide circle over the lower end of the field. It seemed joyful and inspiring, yet every time they flew, Joe felt disappointment. He could walk like a turkey. He could eat like a turkey. He could even talk like a turkey. But he couldn't fly. He considered this a serious handicap in his intense study of wild turkeys. In his dreams, he sometimes imagined that he was flying.

LEARNING NEW THINGS

When Joe almost stepped on a pygmy rattler, he jumped to one side and gave an alarm *putt*. The turkeys followed him but then quickly returned with only a bit of caution. A pygmy rattler was no longer big news to them, and Joe was embarrassed by his overreaction. Later they found a shed rattlesnake skin by the pile of rotten logs and a black racer trying to conceal itself under a pine bough. No snake was able to hide from them, and no snake seemed like a terrible threat.

Early Monday, August 12, Joe heard more turkey vocabulary as he trudged along in darkness toward the pen. The loudest was a very strong *yelp* coming from the turkeys as they anxiously waited for sunrise and the start of their day. He called it the "tree yelp." When Joe arrived, some plopped to the ground and started the happy dance. To him the turkeys were glowing with an ancient flame that bathed him in warmth and energy. Soon he felt inspired to become a man in search of a grasshopper and joined them in a sweeping grasshopper hunt. They raided the north end of the field while he watched. Then they were off to relax at the hammock at Bert's Branch and watch pileated woodpeckers hunt for grubs in a dead oak tree.

Now when they were out, Joe wore his camouflage clothing and tried to stay invisible. The turkeys wandered quite a distance from him, and Joe could see that they needed him less and less. One day he would be alone. But not yet. When they returned to the pen, the turkeys insisted that Joe stay with them until lightning forced him inside.

A DIFFERENT IMPRINTING EXPERIENCE

JOE HAD A LOT of experience imprinting with wild animals. He had tried this process with pocket gophers, cotton rats, flying squirrels, gray squirrels, fox squirrels, gray foxes, red foxes, coyotes, bobcats, raccoons, possums, white-tailed deer, a macaque monkey, wood ducks, quail, crows, numerous songbirds, hawks, owls, and to some extent with reptiles, although he felt they really did not imprint on anything except perhaps food. He had shared his bed with these creatures as a good way to get to know their wild nature. He knew for a fact that a raccoon would always prefer a warm bed and a pecan cookie to a hollow log and a frog.

The adventure with the wild turkeys was different. For the first time, he was trying to keep an imprinted animal's experience separate from his human life. He chattered with turkey talk, shared turkey interests, and attempted to do things as turkeys would prefer. He did not bring them into his yard, near the cabin, or close to his truck. When they were out on long adventures, they never saw another human being, not even Claudia. He didn't feed them directly from his hand. He wanted to experience their true nature and felt that the experiment was going better than expected.

Before the wild turkey imprinting, Joe had spent much time observing, painting, drawing, hunting, photographing, and reading about wild turkeys. He thought he knew a lot about them but as the experiment progressed, he realized that he had so much more to learn. His life as a turkey opened up a new level of sensory detail and understanding.

Wild turkeys were very clever, highly complex, and extremely curious. They had a tremendous ability to detect movement from a great distance. They could see and hear well and didn't miss a thing. They were always gathering important information about their surroundings.

In all his animal studies, Joe had never come across a creature that made such an effort to know and understand everything around them.

As he watched them browsing far in the distance, he knew that the imprinting experience had not affected their interactions with the environment. One day soon, their desire to be on their own would be stronger than their need for him.

Would they look back or just wander away and leave him to walk alone?

CHAPTER 13

Fowl Pox and a Playdate

ALMOST LIKE CHICKEN POX

ON WEDNESDAY, AUGUST 14, fowl pox started to show up as sores on the heads and faces of the turkeys. Some had a few sores; others had many. Joe knew that this was all part of the wild turkey experience but hoped that none would get too sick and that no sores would get infected.

When they took a walk to the old field, it was beginning to look like autumn. Brilliant purple and yellow flowers were starting to pop out. Most of the fruits were gone, and the grasses, like broom and deer tongue, were growing tall. The fruits of the paw paw trees had gone to seed, but cocoons for the next season's zebra swallowtail butterflies were on the leaves. In the damp areas at the edges, Joe enjoyed all the yellow swamp sunflowers, which he thought were the most beautiful sunny things ever.

The turkeys tried to eat the pods of rabbit bells, but most were too hard and dry. They were very excited about the triangular seedpods of a plant called beggar lice. As Joe walked near them, the dense hairs on the sticky little pods stuck to his jeans and boots. The turkeys pecked them off for a high-protein meal.

The turkeys continued to talk about nearby resident wild turkeys, but Joe did not always see them. He could hear their loud *putt putt putts* and knew that the voices of the two groups were the same. He also could recognize their tracks, which were smaller than those of his flock. But the turkeys did not express a desire to meet and Joe felt like his presence might be preventing this. He continued to wear camouflage hoping that the resident turkeys wouldn't notice him.

SWEET PEA GETS SICKER

Saturday, August 17, was another workday for Joe, with lots of rain. There were no complaints from the turkeys, however, as they stayed in the pen to dust, preen, and practice aggressive fighting behavior. Fowl pox was spreading.

By Sunday, just about everyone had it. Most of them behaved as if they were fine, but a few looked quite pitiful.

Sweet Pea suffered the most. She looked and acted sick, with sores covering her head and even her feet.

However all were able to go out for a walk. Joe was the first to reach Bert's Branch and was delighted to see a beautiful hooded warbler in a myrtle tree. Rich black feathers covered its neck and breast and much of its head, surrounding its yellow face like a hoodie. Other parts were pale yellow and olive green.

Hooded warbler

Over and over, the bird twitched its tail to expose white spots underneath. This attracted attention like a flashbulb. Sometimes a hummingbird would fly up close, looking like it wanted to chase the warbler away. After watching for a while, Joe finally figured out this behavior. The warbler was so colorful that the hummingbird thought it was a flower—it looked like a possible food source.

As they walked along the Branch, Joe saw the tracks of a black bear, deer, and raccoon, and of wild turkeys all together on a sandbar. He tried not to add his boot tracks to the mix. In the wild, he preferred not to see human footprints, even if they were his own.

Two red-shouldered hawks put the turkeys, who were some distance from Joe, on alert. When one of the hawks moved in close, Joe thought the turkeys would panic and give the alarm *putt*. But the turkeys made no effort to hide. They fanned their tails and fluffed their feathers. They had outgrown these hawks and stood up against them. Finally a noisy jay chased off the hawks.

On the way back, Joe walked his usual two or three miles, while the turkeys walked even more as they zigged and zagged. In the heat and humidity, it was always a strenuous workout. They found another resident turkey feather, too big for any turkey to eat. Joe dropped it when he picked up a dead gopher tortoise shell that they often inspected. It was starting to deteriorate in the weather, so he decided to add it to his collection.

BACK-AND-FORTH TURKEY TALK

On Monday, August 19, they returned to pick up the feather. They encountered the largest pygmy rattlesnake Joe had ever seen, but the turkeys were more interested in investigating tortoise bones. Then they enjoyed plump gallberry fruit because the deerberries were almost gone. Joe ate a few and found them less tart than deerberries but with a flavor similar to oversteeped tea. Like grasshoppers, he thought they were best left for the turkeys, who now had purple mouths from the juice.

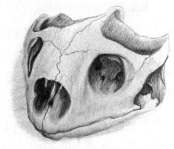

Tortoise skull

Wednesday, August 21, had a record low temperature of 61°F. This was in the aftermath of Hurricane Bob, the worst hurricane of the 1991 season. When they returned to the Branch, Joe enjoyed a cool rest under a water oak tree until his ears picked up a sound. What was that?

Everyone was startled to hear *putts* and *yelps* coming from the swampy area. It was the resident wild turkeys. Joe and his flock answered with *purrs, putts,* and *trills,* and all were very interested. Some young turkeys began to head toward the activity downstream.

A resident wild turkey came closer, making a loud musical *yelp yelp yelp.* Then two others from that group moved up and responded with *pit pit.* This was followed by the loud flapping of many wings and more *yelps* from the swamp. Joe and the young turkeys now realized that a large number of resident wild turkeys were nearby.

Resident turkeys walked up the creek while Joe's turkeys walked down. They were finally meeting face-to-face. It was a tense moment for Joe. He had no idea what would happen.

The three residents who walked up to investigate were not too interested. They ate quietly.

The young turkeys watched them with intense curiosity. Then some began to ignore the strangers and go back to eating. The playdate was going very slowly. For an hour, Joe tried not to move a muscle. The resident wild turkeys stayed in the hammock. There was a lot of wild turkey talk from both groups, although Joe thought his turkeys sounded rather shy.

Suddenly a fourth resident turkey tramped through a gallberry thicket to the edge of the creek. She made a loud, startling *cackle!* It was a distressing sound, and the other three turkeys hurried away.

The young turkeys raced back to Joe and huddled quietly by his side. As they continued to scan the hammock, Joe thought they could still hear the resident turkeys, although he could not. Eventually they relaxed and went back to preening and eating and other normal behavior.

Joe was disappointed. Why had that fourth turkey been so rude and insistent? Had she seen him under the camouflage?

NO WORRIES

As they returned to the pen, they came across many fresh signs of resident turkey activity. The turkeys investigated and pecked at all the small feathers. Joe noticed, as usual, that the birds were not frustrated or worried. They were curious and excited and not interested in changing a thing. They always enjoyed whatever they were doing, as if they simply loved being alive.

This left Joe feeling optimistic. His experiment was going well with a group that liked to participate. It was a nice reward for his months of dedicated work, dawn to dusk and seven days a week.

Thursday, August 22, was another cool day. There were fewer gnats, and with lower temperatures, no snakes had been sighted recently either. It seemed like a great moment to explore new territory. They entered a bay swamp with thickets of wild azalea, gallberry, doghobble, and titi trees. In a dark corner, they found an old terra-cotta turpentine pot. It was not broken or even cracked. The turkeys found it interesting but decided it was not a wild turkey thing. They chose to leave it undisturbed, along with the box turtle hiding nearby.

As they looked for food, they found more evidence of the resident wild turkeys. In fact, these turkeys had already browsed the area for grass seeds, especially the panic grass, which was a favorite. They were also competing for the few remaining deerberries and blueberries. So were the foxes, as Joe saw their tracks and droppings in many places.

DOG DANGER

THE NEXT DAY Joe took a 30-minute lunch break at the cabin during a rain shower. When he came back to the porch to put on his boots, he saw a large red Doberman pinscher. He jumped up and chased after it with a shoe. The unidentified dog bolted into the field.

Then Joe raced to the pen and was shocked at the scene. The turkeys were limp and bloody, wandering about as if in a daze. The dog hadn't been able to get in, but the turkeys had injured themselves. In panicked flight, they banged into the wire walls. Paw Paw lay dead in the corner. She had a small wire cut on her head but probably also had a broken neck or internal injury. Sweet Pea, still sick with fowl pox, now seemed in even worse condition. Joe was simply heartbroken.

The young males, the heaviest, had also sustained many cuts as they banged into the wire with their big and powerful bodies. Two could hardly stand, and another was shaky.

Joe added medication to their water and examined their injuries. He found cuts and abrasions but no broken bones. The turkeys wanted to lie close to him and sleep. He stayed very late and buried Paw Paw in the cemetery in one of the brown towels from the incubator.

Three survivors, Sweet Pea, Turkey Boy, and Starker, were unable to fly up to roost. Joe stayed in the pen for several more hours as rain continued to fall. When the grounded turkeys were under the dry roof, he went to the cabin but came back often to check. He expected to find another dead turkey and was relieved when he did not.

On Saturday, August 24, the turkeys mostly wanted to sleep. Some were limping, but the blood on their faces had dried up. Sweet Pea seemed to be doing fairly well, and Samara, always so well groomed, had a deep gash on her head, but it was healing. Now Joe knew that the turkeys were too heavy and strong to be in the pen. It had become a deadly hazard. He asked his neighbors for miles around if anyone knew the dog, but it was a stranger to all and was never seen again.

The next day everyone had improved, although they still wanted to sleep. They were sad to have lost a sibling, and Joe was sad too. To him, each turkey was different and special. He felt like he had lost a friend.

There was less rain in the afternoon, and they made a low-energy outing. After a while, muscles were stretched, talking returned, and everyone was hungry again. Soon they were enjoying such delights as crickets, gallberries, grasshoppers, and peas.

They surrounded a black racer. After that, they chased a large rattlesnake into a gopher tortoise burrow. They jeered into the blackness and dusted away its tracks with their dust baths.

The turkeys were back to normal, and by the next day, most of them had recovered. But Joe had a dilemma. How could he get the turkeys to spend the night outside the pen? And when this happened, would they be safe?

CHAPTER 14

Taking Off

LOOKING AT TREE LIMBS

Monday, August 26, cracked with thunderstorms all day. The turkeys had recovered well from the trauma with the dog. Joe took out his camera and snapped a photo of a hen that had just molted her last juvenile tail feather. Similar to a first grader losing her first tooth, this was a very important event for a four-month-old bird. Like the others, she was almost at her first winter plumage, when they all would have the look of a fully grown wild turkey.

The next day they waited through more thunderstorms and then finally took a late walk. As always Joe tried to do this even if the outing was short. They had some brief moments of browsing, and it was almost dark when they returned home.

Joe entered the pen. For the first time ever, the turkeys did not follow him! They wandered around looking at trees and talking about tree limbs. Joe watched and listened to the turkey talk. It seemed like they had a plan. But what?

A turkey flew up into a tree. With a lot of chatter, others flew up too. This was followed by limbing behavior and lots more talk. And then they roosted. High above, where Joe could not join them, they settled down for the night on the limbs of the tall pines.

Joe had been wondering how to make the transition to roosting outside the pen, and the birds had made the decision for him. They had picked just the right moment.

Joe watched and listened to faint *putts* and *trills* as their heads bobbed slowly in the darkness. They were spread out, two or three turkeys in a tree. One last jake wandered on the ground until he, too, finally decided on a tree far off by the field.

Joe thought about a time when he was a boy watching a similar flock of wild turkeys roosting on a cold winter evening. Then he had known where to find them on the next day's hunt. Now he realized that, as a young hunter, he hadn't been so interested in food. What he'd really wanted was to interact with something that enchanted and mystified him.

As he watched the young turkeys on their first night

in the trees, he knew them better than he could ever have imagined. But this was a big change.

Joe felt left out.

When it was completely dark and the turkeys were quiet, he gave a soft lost call: *kee kee*. They reassured him that no one, with the possible exception of Joe, was lost.

Later he had a dream about being with a large flock of adult turkeys. He asked an elegant hen if she was human imprinted. She said no. Then Joe shyly mentioned that he didn't expect her to know who he was but he had been involved with a large family of human-imprinted turkeys. The turkey looked deep into his eyes and said, "Oh, we know who you are." Then she rejoined the flock.

Joe woke up feeling like he had received a great compliment but also worried that he might be losing his mind.

WOULD THEY STILL KNOW WHO HE WAS?

The next day, before sunrise, Joe sat on the ground below the roosting turkeys with a cup of hot coffee. He'd brought a backpack full of food. As the sky brightened, he could hear *putt putt putt putt* coming from above. With yet more light, the turkeys got very excited. Soon they were noisy with chatter and flying from tree to tree.

Joe moved closer to the field and made three soft *yelp*

Red-shouldered hawk

yelp yelps. Would they respond to his call? Would they still join him for a walk? How much had changed?

The air filled with flapping turkeys as they flew near Joe, some so close and fast that it seemed frightening. Soon they were all gathered around him in an area heavy with dew and tattered spiderwebs. As the turkeys wandered about with their tails held high above the wet grass, Joe knew they had enjoyed a more restful night than he.

They started to walk in the direction of a large buck whose velvety antlers glowed in the light. When the sun touched the tops of the trees, the turkeys found a few gallberries to eat, although many had already been browsed by others.

Soon it got quite hot and they headed toward the hammock and found a cool spot to relax. An aggressive red-shouldered hawk showed up but the turkeys did not panic. They spread their tails wide and held their ground. Joe, in his camouflage, did not move. As the hawk peered at the turkeys from different limbs, Joe made an alarm *putt*. The turkeys ignored it completely. They kept their attention on the hawk until it flew away. Then they relaxed. And Joe relaxed too.

The turkeys began to scan the bay swamp and trees for signs of the resident wild turkeys. They found feathers and other evidence. Later, they encountered a black racer. As usual this fast snake did not run away but faced the turkeys. Joe continued to be fascinated by this behavior because if he were on his own, the snake would run or hide. With the turkeys, he got an opportunity to observe the snake closely.

HAPPY BIRTHDAY!

Thursday, August 29, was Joe's birthday. He celebrated with the turkeys, who ate as many grasshoppers as possible in his honor. And for added pleasure there was a small breeze and no biting gnats.

They flushed out a resident wild turkey that flew into the bay swamp on upper Bert's Branch. Later they heard her *yelp yelp* from the same area. Joe answered with soft *putts* and *yelps*. The young turkeys were fascinated but cautious. Joe made a faint lost call. The young turkeys gave a soft response that was not loud enough to be heard upstream.

The resident hen moved around them with *yelps* and sharp *putts*. She kept heading north with more *yelps* until finally they heard no more. Then all the turkeys fell asleep.

The next day was very hot and the turkeys were in a resting mode. As Joe led the way, he surprised a large coach whip that reared up like a cobra. Then it attacked him with an open mouth. Joe jumped back quickly to avoid getting bitten.

Later he heard a hen *putt* to point out a rattlesnake. Most turkeys continued to forage, but Joe decided to take a look. He saw a two-foot curvy stick lying in the grass. He wondered how an almost fully grown wild turkey could make such a mistake. Joe told her she was silly while she continued to alarm *putt*. Joe almost reached into the grass to grab the stick and show her the error. Then he reconsidered. Next to the stick was a tightly coiled rattlesnake. The hen looked at him, and her next *putt putts* sounded a bit like a scolding *tsk-tsk*.

When a red-shouldered hawk joined them again in the hammock, Joe tried an experiment. He used his voice that sounded like an old dying mouse. The hawk flew in closer. The turkeys spread their tails but they were not impressed. As the hawk moved away, they continued to eat. Two weeks earlier, this would have been a major crisis. Now only a rare great horned owl could be a possible threat to them.

JUST ANOTHER BIRD

AS THE TURKEYS got more and more independent Joe reflected on their remarkable relationship. Sometimes he was a teacher but often he was a student. They would stop all activity to get him to drop behavior that they found confusing. Wrong color? Wrong food? Wrong language? Inappropriate reaction?

Once he made the corrections, they could all go back to being wild turkeys, curious and joyful. And when everything clicked, Joe was just another bird, experiencing the most intimate and deep moments of his life. He couldn't photograph it, he could hardly write about it, yet he knew something was happening that was highly unusual.

As he continued to live his incredible life as a turkey, he wondered—how long would this last?

CHAPTER 15

Odds of Survival

TURKEY HISTORY

GROWING UP AS A WILD TURKEY can be a real challenge.
Everything starts with a good nest. Because it is on the
ground, it needs to be well hidden. An ideal spot would
be under a tree with a grassy field nearby. Then the hen
could get to food easily while incubating the eggs, and
hatchlings wouldn't have to go far to snatch up their first
food. In the world today, with logged forests and plowed
grasslands, good hidden spots can be hard to find.

If the hen locates a site, she will lay one egg per
day for about 11 days. The eggs will be covered with
fallen leaves and pine needles until she starts to sit.
Unfortunately 50 percent of all nests will be either

destroyed or abandoned. Who finds these hidden nests? Raiders include raccoons, foxes, skunks, possums, crows, snakes, squirrels, and humans.

Of the eggs that survive, some will be infertile. Many will hatch, but unfortunately, 70 percent of the poults will not last two weeks. Only a few turkeys will be wise enough, clever enough, and mostly lucky enough to grow up. If they do, they might survive for five or six years or possibly even twice that long. Who are the turkey hunters? They include coyotes, bobcats, raccoons, snakes, weasels, eagles, owls, hawks, and humans.

Wild turkeys are native to North America. Many hundreds of years ago, they had a population of at least seven million. With the continual arrival of settlers from Europe, turkeys were almost wiped out by human turkey hunters, the destruction of forests, and the plowing of grasslands. Delicate plants couldn't grow, and food sources were gone. By 1949, wild turkeys had disappeared from 19 states and were in trouble in most areas where they could still be found. Efforts were made to replace them with domestic farm-raised turkeys, but they didn't have the skills to survive.

Finally in the 1940s–'50s, other efforts were made to protect wild turkeys. Hunting was restricted, and habitat was left alone or restored. Then wild turkeys could be trapped and released to places where they had lived before. Today they *gobble, purr, kee kee,* and *yelp* in the millions once again. Yet every wild turkey faces the harsh reality of survival. Consider the odds.

WEARING DOWN

THE LOSSES IN JOE'S FLOCK were heartbreaking but still 14 turkeys from the original 29 incubated eggs were growing up clever and curious around him. He was simply in awe of his wild turkeys. But they had so many challenges ahead. How long could they survive on their own?

Joe was facing his own challenges. He'd started to get tired in May when he took on the care of so many eggs and hatchlings, and now he was really wearing down. He was often hungry and sleep deprived. It was hot, humid, and rainy, so his clothing was damp most of the time. He wanted to take good notes, but usually found himself scribbling ideas quickly in the field with turkeys underfoot or climbing and sleeping all over him.

At night he tried to organize and make sense of all his scribblings. If the pages were smudged with bloody marks, he knew it had been a bad day for mosquitoes. He wanted his field notes to be in good form so they could later become a book about this experience. Meanwhile he felt like a tired student with not enough time for a science project, math problems, and soccer practice too.

Needing a change, Joe focused on the joy he felt simply being with these wild turkeys. He spent less time talking Turkey and recording in his notebook and more just being curious about whatever was in front of him. Words didn't seem important, nor did thoughts or judgments.

His human identity moved to the background as he lived through this time of being so close to another species. As Joe moved deeper into his life as a turkey he found himself living more like them and less like a human.

Joe was looking at the world with new eyes.

SWEET PEA STAYED WITH JOE

ON SATURDAY, AUGUST 31, the turkeys chased crows from a field where Joe had scattered cracked corn. Then they enjoyed the feast for themselves. They spent the next few days discovering new foods like ripe persimmons and acorns under the oak trees. They also came across a new trail, worn down by animals, that led to the old field. As they explored, Joe enjoyed the fritillary butterflies and fall flowers simply because they were there.

A few days later, they again tried to chase off the crows. This time the birds stood their ground. The turkeys *yelped* and the crows cawed, but they refused to leave. It was a noisy standoff, and the turkeys ended up widely scattered over 10 acres.

Gulf fritillary butterfly

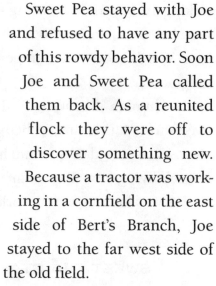

Flight feather

Sweet Pea stayed with Joe and refused to have any part of this rowdy behavior. Soon Joe and Sweet Pea called them back. As a reunited flock they were off to discover something new. Because a tractor was working in a cornfield on the east side of Bert's Branch, Joe stayed to the far west side of the old field.

Joe tried to get an apple eaten before two turkeys could take too many bites. Then he heard a violent fight. All were involved except Sweet Pea, who ran to him. It was their first close meeting with the resident wild turkeys. They ran off when they spotted Joe. Some of his turkeys ended up with lost tail feathers and cuts. Sweet Pea continued to disapprove of all this activity. Joe knew her so well. She was a lover, not a fighter.

When things calmed down, and with Sweet Pea sleeping in his lap, Joe thought about turkey behavior. He liked the way they never looked into the future, unlike humans, who were goal oriented. Turkeys knew how to focus on the moment. They were always where they were supposed to be, looking at opportunities right in front of them. They saw a rattlesnake as something to be understood, not something underfoot. Joe wanted to absorb this way of looking at the world so he let them lead the way. He called this "wild turkey speed."

Joe also thought about the passage of time for wild turkeys. While humans spent years trying to learn all that they needed to know, turkeys already had something in them as ancient as the mountains. Yet they also existed in the moment, like wind in your face. They quickly knew how to peck, talk, eat, and fly, but they were unpredictable and hard to get to know. It was puzzling and mysterious, and Joe called this "wild turkey time."

Suddenly Joe stopped reflecting when he realized that it was far too quiet. He made a soft *yelp*, but there was no answer. He tried a lost call. *Kee kee.*

Only Sweet Pea responded. *Kee?* She was quite concerned. Something was happening that was very different.

Where was everyone? Where were her brothers and sisters?

Finally they spotted the turkeys out in the field

recently mowed by a tractor. Sweet Pea was relieved but Joe was not. He gave an assembly call. The turkeys *yelped* and chattered, but they did not follow him back to the hammock. Instead they headed east.

Joe tried to turn them around and felt frantic because they would not follow. This was something he had always been able to provide for them—the safe areas, the lay of the land. But now they wouldn't listen. They were headed toward a farm, yard dogs, and road traffic—a dangerous situation.

Joe tried to move them to new territory. They stayed with him until he gradually headed toward the hammock. Then they refused to follow.

Joe walked along an overgrown roadbed that crossed the north part of Bert's Branch. This time the thirsty and overheated turkeys showed up to enjoy a drink of water. But now what? Could he get them all the way home?

Dragonfly on plant

Joe stood on the west side of the hammock making lost calls but feeling helpless. Once again, they ignored him, and Joe felt sick from the stress of the situation. He tried again and again, and was relieved to see them, finally, at last, follow him back to the pen.

Joe had expected this separation to occur, but not in this way. He was happy to see the flock's developing independence and confidence, but the sorrow in him was deep, like it had opened up old wounds. Things were different, and he would make changes for their independence, but he felt hurt and somewhat betrayed.

And he wondered, would they still let him join them now and then as if he belonged?

CHAPTER 16

Separation

THE DOOR IS ALWAYS OPEN

IN EARLY SEPTEMBER, the turkeys were free to come and go as they pleased. Joe joined them as much as possible—not because they needed Joe but because Joe needed them. For a while he kept one hen in the pen so he could care for her. She had a deep cut on top of her head with a slight infection. Other turkeys volunteered to stay with her so she wouldn't be alone. With rotating turkeys in the pen, the others decided to stay close to Wren Nest too. At night they roosted in nearby trees.

Joe and the turkeys developed a new and different relationship. He joined them in the mornings, evenings, and when they took walks to browse, but he was no longer the mother. They were more like brothers and sisters.

THE MARVELS OF AN EGG

On October 15, they all browsed in the old field and saw a black racer in a clump of wax myrtles that everyone basically ignored. Then as Joe walked through a thick moist bed of leaves, he stepped on something solid. It crunched. He sifted through the pile to find a broken wild turkey egg, protected and hidden since spring. It was not rotten but looked hard-boiled like the four unfertilized eggs from clutch #2. A search of the area revealed no other eggs.

Joe looked at his turkeys and wondered how they could have started from similar eggs to become such marvelous and powerful creatures. He felt like all the notes he had taken were incomplete. He had been with them every day of their lives but it seemed almost as if something had happened while he wasn't looking.

These graceful turkeys were more alert, sensitive, and conscious than he was. They were more intelligent and superior, with millions of years of wisdom behind them. His close study uncovered more questions than answers but Joe accepted that. After all, he loved a mystery, and he would have an amazing one to think about for years to come.

In February, the flock continued to stay close to Wren Nest, although they divided into two groups of gobblers and hens. The 4 males stuck together while the 10 females gradually went off on their own.

As they moved into spring, Joe had new concerns. He wanted to help the males, now called gobblers, survive through the five weeks of the spring hunting season. It was also nesting season. Hunters were not allowed to take hens but sometimes mistakes were made. He hoped the hens would not wander too far looking for nests.

In an effort to keep them all in the immediate area, Joe kept one gobbler and at least two hens in the pen and rotated them often. The turkeys, familiar with this place and feeling safe, liked being in the pen. It was easy to get volunteers. The arrangement also gave Joe a close-up opportunity to observe more about the siblings.

EVIL-EYE STARES AND OTHER BEHAVIOR

OF THE FOUR MALES, Rosey was the dominant one and always had been. He did a lot of strutting and drumming, and was the only male to make a loud, shrill, throaty jumble of sounds called a gobble. Rosey was in charge of all the hens. He was the only male who had the looks of a mature gobbler. He had new features, such as a permanent swelling of the caruncles and a snood that dangled over his beak like a small caterpillar. He had long sharp spurs on his legs, very thick cartilage over his eyes, and extra fatty breast tissue too.

Serious fighting sometimes occurred between

Rosey and one of the other males—Stretch, Turkey Boy, or Starker. These other gobblers still looked like juveniles. They rarely strutted and had little change in the caruncles. Sometimes they fought each other to see who would be second, third, or fourth in the social order.

Head Anatomy of Adult Wild Turkey Gobbler

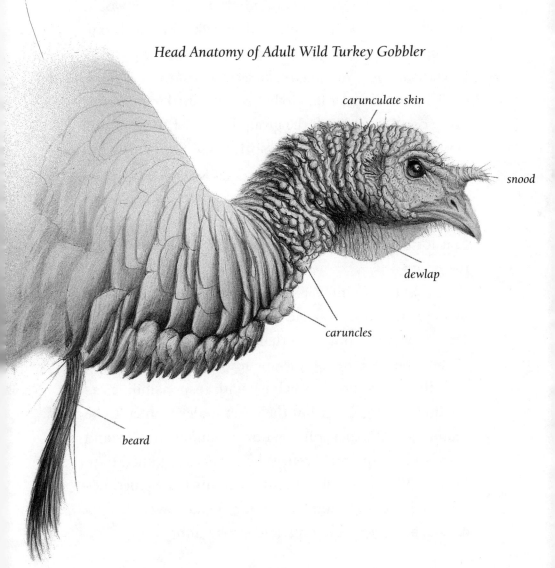

caruncula te skin

snood

dewlap

caruncles

beard

To minimize fighting, which took a lot of energy, the gobblers had a series of signals to help decide who was dominant and who was submissive. Joe called these "evil-eye stares." To indicate that he did not want a fight and would be submissive, a turkey would turn away from an evil-eye stare and lower his head. Then he would back up as far as possible and sit with his neck outstretched low to the ground. In this submissive posture, he was saying, *Okay you can be second, and I will be third.*

This social order had to be reestablished many times every day. If a male left the group for a short time, it was very hard to get back in. One spring day, Starker, always the most handsome of the males, walked off with some resident wild hens for two days. When he returned, looking ruffled and messy, the other gobblers attacked him for several days. Finally he was allowed to rejoin the group.

Joe, at this point, was an observer only and not seen by the males as a rival. He didn't get any evil-eye stares. That, however, would eventually change.

For the time being, Joe spent a lot of time foraging with the males. Rosey was busy with responsibilities as the dominant gobbler but the other males wanted to be around Joe. Whenever he sat down, Starker would stand or sit in his lap and preen. When everyone joined him, Joe had 50 pounds of wild turkey in his lap. Sometimes Stretch liked to stand before Joe, head lowered, eyes closed, and Joe would hold and stroke him.

WANDERING HENS

MOST OF THE HENS stayed close to Wren Nest but a few took off on their own. Claudia received a phone call from a student about a friendly wild turkey in her yard. It was Samara. She allowed Joe to put her into the back of his pickup truck and return five miles to Wren Nest. Then she rejoined her sisters for a few days until she ventured off again. That was the last time Joe saw her.

By the end of April, some hens moved north to the national forest to look for nest sites. Others laid eggs in the pen. Joe blew out the center of these eggs and preserved them in a box.

Sweet Pea and Rosita were the last hens in the pen, and both began to lay an egg every day or so. Joe released them, and as he'd hoped, they nested in the area. After they started to sit on their eggs, he saw them only once or twice a day when they took a short break. Joe followed them so that he would know the general location of their nest sites.

After the second week of incubation, Rosita showed up very nervous and with half her tail missing. Joe followed her back to her nest and discovered broken pieces of eggs and more clumps of feathers. It looked like the work of a coyote or bobcat. Joe hoped she might nest again as some wild hens will try a second or even a third time if things do not go well.

Sweet Pea showed up most days for an easy meal and sometimes took time for lap sitting or preening. After several weeks she stopped coming and Joe suspected that her brood had hatched. He happily imagined her guarding them in a secret thicket, watching out for red-shouldered hawks and slithering rattlesnakes.

CHECKING UP ON SWEET PEA

IN LATE MAY, Joe decided to try to locate Sweet Pea's exact nest site. He knew only that it was near the gallberries on the upper west side of the old field. As he got close, he saw a broken eggshell. A few yards farther, he found more broken shells. Then to his dismay, he spotted the feathers.

He picked up the dried and tattered remains of Sweet Pea and sat with them in his lap. There was a piece of chewed and gnawed wing and some beautiful feathers from the tail and breast. Joe felt limp and profoundly sad. He wondered how he could let himself become so close to creatures that die in such great numbers. He was shocked that their skills could be overcome so quickly. He felt a deep loss for the occupants of the eggs. Had they heard Sweet Pea talk to them? Had she treasured them? Had they felt the warmth of her body and the brightness of the sun?

Somewhere, Joe thought, there might be a den of bright-eyed coyote pups or bobcat kittens that had enjoyed a day without hunger. Sweet Pea was his favorite turkey, but nature has no favorites. Joe calls this the unforgiving game that we have chosen to play, and these are the rules.

CHAPTER 17

Life Without Turkeys

LONELY

ON A SATURDAY in late May, a few days after Joe had found Sweet Pea, the one-year-old gobblers stayed near him, hoping he would join them on an adventure. He was too busy, so they took off to the north without him. For the next week Rosita was the only turkey around. She visited for an hour or so each day but she seemed restless. Soon she was gone too.

For the first time in over a year, since he first got the eggs, Joe was alone. There were no wild turkeys in his life.

He was happy for their independence and also for a return to time for himself. But he felt empty, like the "empty nest" syndrome that parents might experience when their children are grown. He got up early and walked out to the old field toward the national forest. He waited and waited for a familiar face, but none came by. He searched in sandy places for footprints, feathers, and other clues of their activity. He found nothing, not even a hint of the resident wild turkeys.

The vibrant wilderness that he had known, with so many things to discover, now seemed like weeds and scraggly trees, shadows and emptiness. Everything was far too quiet. The coach whip that he had encountered so many times no longer appeared. The cardinals that had liked his company were uninterested and even afraid. The red-shouldered hawks and crows paid him no attention. Even when he walked by the pile of rotten logs, no rattlesnake revealed itself.

Before, he had been allowed a special passage into this world as an accepted companion of the wild turkeys. No one had noticed him. But now he was just another human intruder, and the wildlife stayed hidden. The rich experience of being accepted by the wild turkeys that had known him so well was over. The door that had opened to their wild world had closed. Joe was left with loneliness. Was this the end of his life as a turkey, or would there be more interactions?

A FEW TURKEY SIGHTINGS

FOR WEEKS, no males were seen, and only on a rare occasion would someone in the area report seeing a hen. Then in mid June, while Joe was on an errand, Claudia called to say that one of the males had returned, and it was not Rosey or Starker. It turned out to be Turkey Boy, and he chose to make a long visit at Wren Nest. He and Joe quickly started up new adventures together, reviving a great joy in Joe's life. Turkey Boy also became close to Claudia.

Later in June, a friend reported that two wild turkey hens were on her land in the national forest. Six or seven poults at least eight weeks old were with them. Sometimes they ate near her house but left when she came outside. They stayed until August.

During the summer, Turkey Boy was sometimes with Joe, but occasionally he would walk off with resident wild turkeys for a day or two. He always returned and eventually chose to spend all of his time with Joe. Joe felt that any day without an adventure for the two of them was a missed opportunity for him and a disappointment for Turkey Boy.

Joe thought that thousands of years ago, when turkeys were domesticated, it may have started with a turkey that had a personality like Turkey Boy.

A NEW RELATIONSHIP

JOE AND TURKEY BOY spent almost every day on adventures, and once again Joe was seeing the world through the eyes of a wild turkey. Turkey Boy felt the need to snatch the less dangerous snakes from their hiding places and toss them into the light of day. Joe joined him on hands and knees as they studied creeks and hammocks. Their curiosity led them to things that had been missed in the past. They found so many salamanders—mole, slimy, marbled, and red eft. And plenty of tree frogs—squirrel, green, gray, pinewoods—and spring peepers. It was the business of a wild turkey to know these things.

Common toad

Turkey Boy had his own interests, but if he saw Joe investigating something, he came to take a look. Joe's pile of leaves always seemed more interesting than his own. Besides, Joe could do something quite amazing. He could roll over a rotten log.

The world beneath a decaying log was a whole new experience for Turkey Boy. It could be so colorful, with green fern moss, and red, yellow, and violet mushrooms. Or it might hide a shrew, a salamander, a ground skink, a frog, a toad, a nest of white-footed mice, and fat grubs too. These were all things to wonder about and new food to enjoy. After each rollover, Joe carefully returned the log to its original position.

Turkey Boy and Joe created an incredible new bond. When they turned away from each other, Joe felt an insistent call, a physical tug to get back together again. Turkey Boy called for him often when they were separated. Joe sensed that neither one of them was comfortable when the other was not around.

Turkey Boy roosted in a sweet bay or a slash pine tree close to the cabin at Wren Nest. Sometimes he woke Joe early with a great thump on the cabin roof. When Joe joined him, he was greeted with the "happy dance" with ducking, dodging, wings outstretched, and a shake of his head. Sometimes he would jump up and touch Joe lightly with his feet.

Joe could hardly disappoint Turkey Boy and tried to join him whenever he could. However, he did have work to do in his studio. During those times, Turkey Boy would browse the hammock, visit the bird feeding station, doze, or preen. But he always kept Joe in sight through the two large windows at the back of the cabin. He attempted to join him through the glass but quickly learned that this was not a good idea.

If Joe left Wren Nest, Turkey Boy tried to follow. So Joe drove up into the old field and then sped back in the other direction, leaving Turkey Boy behind. He clocked Turkey Boy many times and learned that his maximum running speed was 16 miles per hour. Any faster than this and he would flap his wings, fly past Joe like a rocket, and block the trail.

When Joe went jogging around an oval trail in the old field, Turkey Boy came too. He could keep up for about a half mile. Then he figured out a way to run in smaller and smaller circles until he was browsing at the center. He rejoined Joe when he began walking to cool down. Turkey Boy eventually got in better shape and was able to jog a mile, but he never ran faster than 16 miles per hour.

Turkey Boy stayed at Wren Nest for the human company. If Joe or Claudia was not around he walked north to the national forest. When Joe returned and didn't see him in the area, he'd hike up to the forest too. If Turkey Boy was hard to find, Joe *yelped* and made lost calls. Eventually they got back together.

One afternoon in late August, Joe saw two hens from

Mature Turkey Boy

clutch #1 with poults in the field of cracked corn. He counted twelve or thirteen before everyone started to dash for cover. The hens stayed for a few seconds and then they ran off. Joe whistled a lost call and they stopped for just a moment. Then they continued on after their brood.

The poults were about 10 weeks old with their first basic tail feathers. Joe suspected that they were the result of a second nesting because it was so late in the summer. He hoped one of the hens was Rosita but he couldn't tell for sure and never saw them again.

Turkey Boy, meanwhile, had molted into fully mature feathers. At 16 months, he was as tall as Joe's waist and weighed over 16 pounds. He had a nine-inch tuft of thin feathers called a beard that dangled from his chest. His sharp spurs were over ¾ inch long. Because of the nutritious food he'd received, he was larger than a resident wild turkey and as big as a two-year-old gobbler.

Turkey Boy was also very clever. If Joe took food outside, Turkey Boy assumed it was good food for him too. Joe ended up sharing his morning coffee, noon sandwiches, and an evening sip of wine, which is like liquid berries to a wild turkey. His gritty mouth always left a bit of sand at the bottom of the glass.

Turkey Boy also spent a lot of time with Claudia in the garden, digging, planting, and weeding. Sometimes he did too much thinning of the greens, but she didn't really mind. Claudia whispered "Birdie" when he called softly to her.

One afternoon while Joe was away, Turkey Boy browsed with Claudia on the east side of the old field. Suddenly there was a great commotion and a flapping of wings. Claudia was far ahead but she hurried back toward the uproar. Turkey Boy was running from a large predator, probably a coyote, which disappeared quickly into the hammock. Despite the fact that Turkey Boy spent time with humans, he had remained on wild turkey alert. He lost a pile of beautiful rear feathers but was uninjured. The feathers grew back in about eight weeks.

In late November, perhaps because it was hunting season and with less food in the area, there were no other wild turkeys around. For weeks Turkey Boy didn't disappear into the forest but became more and more fixated on Joe.

All of this was wonderful until January. Then Turkey Boy began to change.

Joe had read that human-imprinted turkeys can become aggressive with humans, so he had feared this could be a possibility. However, this bird had always been gentle and protective with Claudia and all guests and strangers too. He still wanted to be around Joe, but he was no longer gentle and carefree.

In his wildest dreams, Joe couldn't have imagined all that would come next.

Coyote and Turkey Boy

CHAPTER 18

The Tale of Turkey Boy

A STRONG URGE TO FIGHT

THERE WAS NOTHING in Turkey Boy's wild turkey mind to account for a companion that was once a mother, then a friend, and now what? How did Joe fit into his social order? Was he a brother? A rival? If so, then Turkey Boy, who was now 18 pounds with spurs over an inch long, must fight. It was his new mission in life.

One day Joe was pulling up thick gallberry and sweet pepper plants. Usually Turkey Boy loved this activity because it exposed worms, tree frogs, and grubs for him to eat. But Joe noticed his unusual excitement and stopped to find out what was going on.

Turkey Boy stood close and looked him straight in the eye.

Joe felt uncomfortable, spoke calmly, and reached out his hand. Turkey Boy pecked it and drew blood. Joe didn't understand what was happening and reached out again. Turkey Boy pecked hard once more. Joe gave him a shove and asked him what he was doing.

Turkey Boy looked back at Joe as an adversary. It was time to fight.

Joe started for the cabin but a furious Turkey Boy blocked his path. Joe made it inside and Turkey Boy followed him from window to window strutting and drumming. His head was glowing with vivid shades of violet, red, and purple. As Joe ran water over his injury, he realized that his feelings were hurt more than his hand.

Joe thought if he stayed out of sight, Turkey Boy might calm down and forget. But he did not. He was obsessed with having a fight, and he had the strength and sharp spurs to make it serious. Joe was frightened when Turkey Boy, trembling with rage, gave him the evil eye.

Joe thought of a plan to let Turkey Boy know that he could be dominant without a fight. Would that work? Joe ran from the house out into the grassy field and threw himself on the ground in a submissive posture. He covered his head with his arms and hands. Turkey Boy ran after him, jumped on his body, and pecked and pulled at his clothes. Then the furious bird pulled off his cap and shook it violently up and down. This almost made Joe laugh until the bird started to stab and gouge him with his powerful beak.

Joe tried all the tactics that helped the other gobblers avoid a fight but the message did not get through. The attack continued as Turkey Boy's anger seemed to have no limit. Finally, with hands and ears bleeding, Joe ran back to the cabin. Turkey Boy chased him.

When Joe left the cabin later to jog, Turkey Boy attacked him as he ran by. Joe tried to ignore him and turn away, but nothing worked. This was turning into a serious and dangerous problem. Turkeys attack at face level, spurring, pecking, slapping with powerful blows from their wings. This went on for days and Joe knew it had to stop.

One day he broke off a longleaf pine bough and decided to defend himself. He hoped the needles would cushion the blow but he wanted to get Turkey Boy to respect him enough to leave him alone. When Turkey Boy jumped and tried to spur him, Joe swung the bough. At one point, he tripped and fell. Turkey Boy was all over him. Joe got up and swung again. This time the pine bough hit the bird in the head and neck and sent him backward.

With all the vivid color disappearing from his head, Turkey Boy ran off to the north. Joe returned to the cabin bleeding, battered, and tired. He felt like a child who just had a terrible fight with a best friend and lost so much.

The next morning, Turkey Boy returned with the vivid colors back in his face. He was ready for another round. But Joe had already decided there would never be another round. No matter what, he would not have another fight with this wild turkey.

For the next two months, Joe learned how to use various avoidance tactics so that he could enjoy time with Turkey Boy. He never looked him straight in the eye. He did not walk directly toward him. He led, and Turkey Boy followed, and the two of them made a small, familiar flock. Long walks to new territories could distract Turkey Boy for a time. But once they returned to the cabin, Joe needed to rush inside to avoid the return of the bird's anger and aggression.

TURKEY BOY GETS SICK

JOE TRIED SOME MEDICINE to calm down Turkey Boy but it seemed to have no effect. Then in early April, Claudia saw Turkey Boy standing under a pine tree. He looked deathly sick and barely able to stand. The night before he had been in perfect condition. Joe got him back to the pen and filled the waterer with diluted Terramycin. But Turkey Boy would not eat or drink. He backed up into the corner and lay down.

Joe wondered if he had caught something from new domestic fowl in the neighborhood, possibly blackhead disease caused by a parasite. He got some medicine and vitamins from the veterinarian but thought that unless the injections worked quickly, Turkey Boy would not survive. Joe had to hold him down for three shots, and the bird managed to fight back with a great deal of strength. Joe wouldn't let Claudia help with the struggle because he didn't want Turkey Boy to connect her with all this sickness, fear, and pain.

The next morning Turkey Boy panicked when Joe showed up with another syringe. It was so much effort and trauma to give the injection that Joe decided to stop and let Turkey Boy fight this in his own way.

He lay in the back corner for nearly three weeks, feverish and too sick to fight off the gnats. His head turned black from disease, and he lost half of his body weight. He was able to eat a few greens that Claudia brought for him.

After three weeks he showed signs of recovery as he scratched the floor of the pen looking for food. Joe gave him the high-protein food that he hadn't eaten since he was a poult. He gulped it down and gradually the scabs and discoloration of his head disappeared.

This remarkable bird had beaten the odds.

CHANGES FOR TURKEY BOY

TWO DAYS LATER, Joe coaxed him out of the pen with a handful of greens. Turkey Boy was a bit nervous but no longer showed any aggression toward him. They went out to the field and found the nearest gopher tortoise burrow. Joe lay on the ground while Turkey Boy joyfully dusted and preened in the loose dirt.

Eventually Turkey Boy grew strong and healthy, and when he saw Joe he did the happy dance once again. But he no longer gobbled in the mornings, never strutted, and the bright aggressive colors were gone from his head. Joe didn't know if this was a delayed reaction to the medicine or a lingering effect from the disease.

Turkey Boy went through another change too. He became more independent and no longer saw Joe as the main focus of his life. Gradually he made his way up into the forest as resident turkeys returned to the area. By late April, Joe hadn't seen Turkey Boy for several weeks and hadn't spotted any of his other turkeys for months.

Joe missed them all. On many days, he took long hopeful walks in the forest. He saw signs of foxes, coyotes, raccoons, armadillos, crows, beetles, ant lions, and snakes. But the turkey family that he had known so well was gone. All the physical, mental, and emotional stress of the last two years was deflated. He felt a deep loneliness as he missed this connection with another species.

Joe didn't want to go back to a life without turkeys. For a while he found it very difficult to become interested in other things. But he eventually turned his two-year collection of daily journals and many illustrations into a book. *Illumination in the Flatwoods* was published in 1995. He later went to Wyoming and made intense studies of bighorn sheep and mule deer, and wrote about these also.

Joe would always feel the spirit of the flock and his incredible experience of living life as a turkey. Someday he hoped to lean against a gnarled oak tree and have an old bird answer his call. Something would be familiar, and the bird would linger for a few moments as they exchanged a subtle message. Joe would say, "I know you, old friend. I recognize you by your iridescence, your incandescence, your illumination. I recognize you by your loneliness. You must be my brother."

Glossary

BROODER BOX. A safe, warm container for poults after they hatch, dry out, and are ready to leave the incubator. A lightbulb provides warmth. Waterers and feeders are added for food and drink. Sawdust or towels can be used over the floor.

CANDLING. Observing eggs in front of a strong light to see the stage of development in an embryo.

CARUNCLES. Fleshy bumps on the head, neck, and throat of the turkey. Both males and females have them. When males get excited during courtship, the caruncles, dewlap, and snood can fill with blood and change from a pale color to bright red or blue.

CLUTCH. A set of eggs laid and incubated by a hen. For turkeys, this is usually 4 to 17 eggs.

DEWLAP. A fleshy flap of skin that is attached to the throat and neck of a turkey. Often but incorrectly called a "wattle."

EMBRYO. An unhatched poult (or any unborn animal) in the process of development.

FLATWOODS. A woodland terrain that is flat and low. The soil is sandy. Sometimes it is flooded, sometimes dry. In Florida, the tallest trees in the flatwoods are evergreen pines with long needles. The lower shrubs include blueberries and pointy palmettos. Tall grasses cover the ground.

FLIGHT FEATHER. A long, strong asymmetrical feather from the wing with one side wider than the other.

Fowl pox. A highly contagious viral disease in birds around the world. It is similar to chicken pox in humans and not too hard to treat unless an open sore gets infected.

Gobble. A loud, descending throaty jumble of sounds made by a male turkey.

Imprinting. A process where a young animal recognizes another animal, person, or thing as its parent.

Incubator. A closed box with heat and humidity controls to protect eggs when no hen is around to sit on the nest.

Jake. A male turkey older than a poult until it becomes a gobbler at six months of age.

Pip. To peck the first tiny hole in an eggshell before hatching using a temporary "egg tooth" on the beak.

Poult. A very young turkey.

Precocial. Any animal born alert, aware, and ambulatory (bird, reptile, or mammal).

Roost. A place where birds regularly gather and settle to rest at night.

Snood. A piece of turkey flesh sticking up from the forehead.

Strutting. A walking behavior in male gobblers with wings dropped low, head tucked back, and tail raised high with feathers spread.

Vector. Any animal or organism that can carry and transmit a disease through its bite. The vector for fowl pox is the turkey gnat. Mosquitoes, ticks, and blackflies are vectors for other diseases.

Yelper. An instrument used by hunters to produce a call or whistle to imitate the yelp of a wild turkey hen.

Bibliography

Becker, John E. *Wild Turkeys*. Farmington Hills, MI: Kid Haven Press, 2003.

Buford, Bill. "Talking Turkey: The man who communicates with gobblers." *New Yorker* (Nov. 20, 2006): 38–47.

Hutto, Joe. *Illumination in the Flatwoods: A Season Living Among the Wild Turkeys*. Guilford, Connecticut: The Lyons Press, 1995.

Lorenz, Konrad. *Here am I–Where are you? The Behavior of the Graylag Goose*. New York: Harcourt Brace & Co., 1988.

Nickens, T. Edward. "Wild Turkey on the Rocks?" *Audubon* (Nov./Dec. 2013): 32–37.

Patent, Dorothy Hinshaw. *Wild Turkeys*. Minneapolis, MN: Lerner Publications, 1999.

Trout, John Jr. *The Complete Book of Wild Turkey Hunting: A Handbook of Techniques and Strategies*. New York: Lyons Press, 2000.

Williams, Lovett E. Jr. *The Book of the Wild Turkey*. Tulsa, OK: Winchester Press, 1981.

http://www.pbs.org/wnet/nature/my-life-as-a-turkey-full-episode/7378/

http://www.pbs.org/wnet/nature/my-life-as-a-turkey-video-a-new-mother/7289/

http://www.pbs.org/wnet/nature/my-life-as-a-turkey-video-grass
hopper-run/7286/

http://www.pbs.org/wnet/nature/my-life-as-a-turkey-qa-with-nat
uralist-joe-hutto/7389/

http://www.pbs.org/wnet/nature/my-life-as-a-turkey-audio-slide
show-recreating-a-life-with-turkeys/7386/

http://www.pbs.org/wnet/nature/my-life-as-a-turkey-whos-your
-mama-the-science-of-imprinting/7367/

http://trib.com/news/state-and-regional/wyoming-naturalist-reflects
-on-experience-as-a-parent-to-wild/article_ed01418a-ee9c-5e72
-8399-120d460ad9fd.html

http://www.dnr.sc.gov/wildlife/turkey/sound/turkeysound_index
.html

http://www.allaboutbirds.org/guide/Wild_Turkey/sounds

http://www2.fcps.edu/islandcreekes/ecology/wild_turkey.htm

http://sfrc.ufl.edu/Extension/florida_forestry_information/forest
_resources/pine_flatwoods.html

entnemdept.ufl.edu/insectid/

Acknowledgments

Thanks to Christy Ottaviano, an incredible editor on this book, Jessica Anderson, Ilana Worrell, and Patrick Collins. And thanks to Joe Hutto for delving into this intriguing experiment and creating a detailed record with journals, illustrations, photos, and a book that can now be shared with new readers.

Index